Equality and Diversity in Further Education

URTHER
DUCATION

You might also like the following books from Critical Publishing

A Complete Guide to the Level 4 Certificate in Education and Training
By Lynn Machin, Duncan Hindmarch, Sandra Murray and Tina Richardson
978-1-909330-89-4
Published September 2013

A Complete Guide to the Level 5 Diploma in Education and Training
By Lynn Machin, Duncan Hindmarch, Sandra Murray and Tina Richardson
978-1-909682-53-5
September 2014

The A–Z Guide to Working in Further Education
By Jonathan Gravells and Susan Wallace
978-1-909330-85-6
Published September 2013

Dial M for Mentor: Critical Reflections on Mentoring for Coaches, Educators and Trainers
By Jonathan Gravells and Susan Wallace
978-1-909330-00-9
Published September 2012

Inclusion in Further Education
By Lydia Spenceley
978-1-909682-05-4
June 2014

The Professional Teacher in Further Education
By Keith Appleyard and Nancy Appleyard
978-1-909682-01-6
Published April 2014

Teaching and Supporting Adult Learners
By Jackie Scruton and Belinda Ferguson
978-1-909682-13-9
June 2014

Understanding the Further Education Sector: A Critical Guide to Policies and Practices
By Susan Wallace
978-1-909330-21-4
Published September 2013

Most of our titles are also available in a range of electronic formats. To order please go to our website www.criticalpublishing.com or contact our distributor, NBN International, 10 Thornbury Road, Plymouth PL6 7PP, telephone 01752 202301 or email orders@nbninternational.com.

Equality and Diversity in Further Education

Sheine Peart

Series Editor Susan Wallace

FURTHER EDUCATION

First published in 2014 by Critical Publishing Ltd

British Library Cataloguing in Publication Data
A CIP record for this book is available from the British Library

ISBN: 978-1-909330-97-9

This book is also available in the following e-book formats:

MOBI ISBN: 978-1-909330-98-6
EPUB ISBN: 978-1-909330-99-3
Adobe e-book ISBN: 978-1-909682-00-9

Cover and text design by Greensplash Limited
Project Management by Out of House Publishing
Printed and bound in Great Britain by Bell and Bain, Glasgow

Critical Publishing
152 Chester Road
Northwich
CW8 4AL
www.criticalpublishing.com

Contents

Meet the author   vi

Meet the series editor   vii

1   Introduction: equality and diversity in Further Education   1

2   Professional responsibilities of tutors in Further Education   5

3   Race and disability in Further Education: international and national perspectives   16

4   Meeting the needs of adult learners   36

5   Working with younger learners and the impact of youth on learning   50

6   Meeting the needs of transient populations   68

7   Working with cross-cultural groups   80

8   Integrating offenders in Further Education   94

9   Managing gender and sexual orientation issues   112

10   Managing equality and diversity in Further Education   128

Glossary of acronyms   143

Index   146

Meet the author

Sheine Peart

I have worked in schools, colleges, local authorities and youth and community settings. I have taught on various vocational programmes, working with challenging students, within Further Education (FE) for 15 years. I held the post of the college equalities manager for eight years and also managed a local authority education team dedicated to raising the achievement of African and Caribbean pupils. In my current post at Nottingham Trent University I teach on the pre-service full-time PGCE, Professional Graduate Certificate in Education, and the Certificate in Education for the Lifelong Learning Sector as well as managing the Masters in Education courses. I am currently engaged in supporting one large urban college in developing a dedicated in-house student support group for Black male students, called 'Black on Track'.

Meet the series editor

Susan Wallace

I am Emeritus Professor of Education at Nottingham Trent University where, for many years, part of my role was to support learning on the initial training courses for teachers in the Further Education (FE) sector. I taught in the sector myself for ten years, including on BTEC (Business and Technology Education Council) programmes and Basic Skills provision. My particular interest is in the motivation and behaviour of students in FE, and in mentoring and the ways in which a successful mentoring relationship can support personal and professional development. I have written a range of books, mainly aimed at teachers and student teachers in the sector, and I enjoy hearing readers' own stories of FE, whether it's by email or at speaking engagements and conferences.

1 Introduction: equality and diversity in Further Education

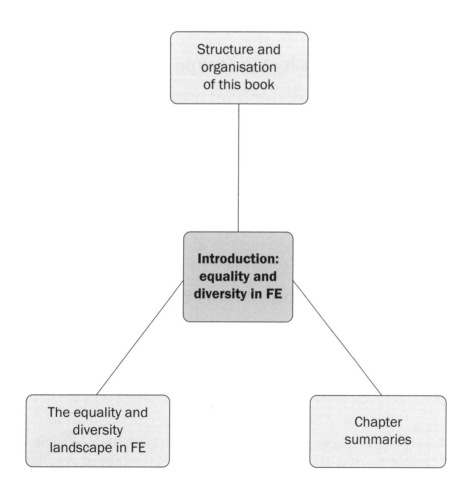

Chapter aims

This book has been written for all staff who work in a teaching, training or supporting learning capacity in Further Education (FE). The overall purpose of this book is to alert you to some of the historic and contemporary discussions regarding equality and diversity and to give you an opportunity to formulate your personal responses to these issues. This book cannot provide an answer to each and every situation you may encounter in your working life. However, the critical thinking tasks and case studies embedded throughout the book will help you to work through how you might manage these issues, where you could go for support and how to build yourself a firm ally base from which you can challenge inequality and discrimination.

The function of this chapter is purely to provide you with a map to navigate the rest of the book. While it is hoped you will want to read the entire book, it is almost inevitable that you will find some chapters more useful than others. Appreciating that FE tutors are busy people with multiple demands on their limited time, this chapter will enable you to make informed decisions regarding which chapters you will read and in what order you need to read them.

The equality and diversity landscape in FE

FE is the most diverse of all education sectors. It welcomes students of all abilities from those working at pre-entry level to students studying degree-level programmes; anyone over the age of 14 can attend college, including adult returners and students who have been excluded from schools, and there is no official upper age limit. This book examines the needs of these groups and extends the diversity debate to enable you to review your role as a tutor when working with different learners.

Effectively managing diversity and promoting equality (a legislative requirement of the 2010 Equalities Act) is a significant challenge for all teaching staff who have been given the responsibility of turning statute into reality, with very little advice. This book provides practical suggestions on how FE tutors can begin to meet these challenges.

Structure and organisation of this book

Each chapter in this book is organised in the same way. This is to support ease of use and to enable you to develop rapid familiarity with the text. All chapters begin with a visual map of the chapter contents. If you have very little time, simply consulting this map may be sufficient for you to decide whether or not you wish to read the chapter. However, the visual maps only provide the briefest information and do not give a detailed description of the chapter sections.

Directly following the map, specific chapter objectives are given. These chapter objectives list the skills you will have developed and knowledge you will have gained by working through the chapter contents. To support you in developing your skills and understanding, embedded throughout each chapter you will find a number of critical thinking tasks, case studies and discussions. Each of these different scenarios is drawn from a real situation or is based on an actual event. While some of these situations may be alien to you personally, they represent the range of different incidents that can occur in a college setting. Reading these case studies and carefully considering how you would respond will equip you to effectively manage similar situations should you encounter them in the future.

The critical thinking tasks are a particularly important feature of each chapter. Based on the information you have been given, the tasks invite you to engage both practically and intellectually with how to handle a particular challenge; you are asked to consider the impact and outcome of actions and events; and, most crucially, what such situations mean for you in the context of your working life. For most of these tasks there is no single right answer. Each answer will be, and should be, contextualised. What may seem appropriate in a large, multi-site general FE college may not be suitable in a small, single site, specialist institution. However, regardless of the location, size or type of college, every FE tutor is legislatively bound by the 2010 Equalities Act to work to promote equality of access for all learners, and to promote positive relationships between different groups of college users.

Each chapter also has at least one discussion. The discussions provide a response to the critical thinking tasks. They are not the only response that could be made and there may be other suitable actions or replies. However, they provide a clear summary of an educationally suitable, equality relevant response.

Chapter reflections at the end summarise the key points of the chapter. You are then invited to assess your own learning using the learning review audit. This tool may also help you to plan your own professional development needs by highlighting any areas where you need to complete more work. If your college has an appraisal system you may choose to take copies of some of these audits to discuss with your managers or peers. To support and encourage your further development a short list of further useful reading and websites is given at the end of each chapter.

Chapter summaries

Chapter 2 begins by explaining the requirements on all tutors working in FE, the legislative requirements imposed on those working in the public sector and by organisations such as Teaching Unions and the Institute for Learning (IfL). The IfL is responsible for conferring Qualified Teacher Learning and Skills (QTLS). While it is not obligatory for FE tutors to gain QTLS, it is advisable because it demonstrates professional commitment and competence, and *from the 1 April 2012, IfL members with QTLS status are also recognised as qualified to teach in schools* (IfL website). The IfL thus remains an important and influential organisation for all teaching staff in FE and its role is discussed in this chapter.

Chapter 3 provides a contextual framework for diversity and equality. International and UK national perspectives and agendas are discussed, and pivotal events such as the Little Rock Nine dispute, the Swann Report, the Warnock Report and the Salamanca Conference are described. Historically it considers the impact of the US Civil Rights movement and the politicisation of race issues. It reviews how these arguments transferred to a UK context and charts how the United Kingdom has edged its way towards embracing a race equality agenda. It reviews the politicisation of organisations for people with disabilities and the changing representations of people with disabilities in education through the lens of empowerment, rights and entitlement.

Adults, that is anyone over the age of 18, form the majority student group in FE colleges. Additionally, many courses in FE are taught on a part-time basis. However, sometimes adult learners appear to be an almost invisible population, with their needs being prioritised below that of the full-time 16 to 18 year-old learners. Chapter 4 examines how you can work to ensure that the distinct needs of adult learners are not overlooked and they are not subsumed into a generic youth based culture.

Younger learners may be transferring to FE straight from school and may be used to a tightly structured environment where their time is strictly managed. Chapter 5 considers the support that younger learners might need in order to make a successful transition from being a child instructed what to do at school, to being a young adult capable of making reasoned, rational decisions. It reviews how to build appropriate professional relationships and your legal responsibilities when working with young people.

Chapter 6 examines the needs of transient student populations. In relation to students in this category, you could be working with a group in September who will have left by November. The very nature of being a temporary student means this group can easily be forgotten and as such is a vulnerable group. Three particular groups are considered in this chapter: apprentices, overseas students, and refugees and asylum seekers. The different needs of each are detailed and information which challenges popular reporting is presented.

Chapter 7 considers the implications of working with different cultural groups. It revisits the definition of a culture and provides contemporary examples of new and emerging cultures. It examines equality legislation and the different characteristics which are protected under UK legislation as well as the opportunities and challenges this poses for education.

Chapter 8 examines tutor responsibilities when working with offenders within a college environment. This chapter considers the organisation and structure of the judiciary and how college users may come into contact with different parts of this organisation. The chapter also considers how tutors might respond to potentially challenging or compromising situations.

Homophobic attitudes are still apparent in general society and in education. Chapter 9 examines how tutors can work in a positive way with college users to challenge negative gender stereotypes and to ensure that the requirements of the 2010 Equalities Act are adhered to.

Chapter 10 discusses managing equality and diversity in colleges. To achieve this task colleges need a fair and transparent management system where the needs of all college users are considered within the context of the legislative framework. This chapter evaluates what this means in practice for college users, how the senior management team needs to structure their response to equality issues, departmental action and individual tutor responses to diversity.

A glossary of all acronyms is provided at the end of the book which explains all abbreviations used in these chapters.

References

IfL (online), *Gaining QTLS or ATLS, Professional Formation.* Available at www.ifl.ac.uk/cpd-and-qtls/
gaining-qtls-and-atls/

2 Professional responsibilities of tutors in Further Education

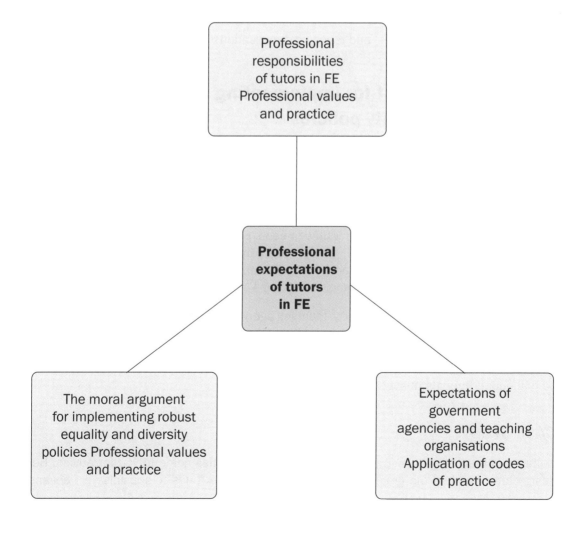

Chapter aims

The purpose of this chapter is to explain your legislative and contractual obligations as a Further Education (FE) tutor in relation to inclusive practice and equality. These are minimum legal requirements. In addition the chapter explores the assumed moral responsibility of FE teachers working in colleges, arguing that it is our professional responsibility as tutors to confront discrimination in all forms and to understand our own assumptions. This may be difficult, but unless we can recognise our attitudes we will not be able to change them or to challenge the actions of others.

When you have finished reading this chapter you will be able to:

- articulate the moral argument for promoting equality and diversity in education;

- identify your contractual obligations as an employee;

- list your professional responsibilities as a tutor in FE;

- list government agencies' and teaching organisations' expectations of FE tutors.

The moral argument for implementing robust equality and diversity policies

Moral arguments have a tendency to polarise opinions, and most people hold firm views on what they believe is right or wrong. While some groups appear to enjoy positive advantages in society, other groups, such as students with disabilities, often have less opportunity. Equality is intimately linked with fairness and providing a means for everyone to participate. Equality is not about treating everyone the same; rather it is recognising specific needs and identifying resources and strategies to meet these needs. Educators are expected to ensure that *all* students regardless of their race, gender, sexuality or other individualised features are given the opportunity to achieve. Education fundamentally challenges the premise that any student is *born to fail* (Wedge and Prosser, 1973, p 1).

Furthermore, each major political party, teaching agencies and other interest groups (including Ofsted) have all agreed on the paramount importance of promoting equality. Ofsted have clarified their position stating that the most effective colleges actively promote *equality and diversity ... through teaching and learning* (Ofsted, 2012, p 7), and therefore equality should be embedded throughout every college's work.

CASE STUDY

Namaan, a practising Muslim female in your tutor group, has come to you for advice. Her design tutor has told the group that he has secured some funds to subsidise a weekend residential trip. Students need only make a small financial contribution. The trip will be from Friday afternoon until Sunday evening and accommodation will be in a small, private hostel with all meals included. The trip is not compulsory and the design tutor has assured the students that if they cannot attend, it will not affect their project grades, although he believes it will be an ideal opportunity to work together. Namaan has investigated the hostel where they will be staying on the web, which states *unfortunately, this small hostel cannot accommodate special dietary requirements, though residents are welcome to prepare their own meals in the hostel kitchen*. Namaan wants to go on the residential and has finally persuaded her family to allow her to attend. As a practising Muslim Namaan will only eat halal food and is unwilling to consume the hostel meals. She is not confident the hostel kitchen will have a suitable food preparation area and even if it did, Namaan feels it is unfair that she should be separated from her friends. She says it makes her seem odd. Namaan feels angry and upset and asks you what she should do.

Critical thinking activity

» *What is your response to this situation?*

» *Has the tutor acted appropriately when sourcing accommodation?*

» *Is Namaan acting reasonably? After all, this is not a compulsory residential.*

Discussion: residential trip

Residential trips can be fantastic learning opportunities. Staff and students can see each other in different environments and often such trips result in improved staff/student relationships. Residential trips are hard work for staff involved, but usually produce positive outcomes.

Residential trips are increasingly rare in FE and the design tutor probably feels pleased he has secured funds to subsidise this one. However, he has not fully thought through all the implications. Although student project grades will not be affected through non-attendance, the trip is not accessible to all students as different dietary requirements cannot be accommodated. It is not a solution that students are told to prepare their own food in the hostel kitchens. Furthermore, the kitchen may not have utensils or food preparation boards which have not been contaminated by forbidden (haram) foods. This would mean Namaan would be unable to eat in the hostel. One of the objectives of any residential is to allow staff and students the opportunity to socialise and integrate. Directing a student to prepare their meals apart from the rest of the group does not promote social integration and as Namaan states, makes her seem 'odd'.

If a tutor wishes to organise a residential, it needs to be fully accessible to all students. This means that necessary access arrangements and dietary needs should be accommodated. If this cannot be guaranteed, then an alternative venue should be sought. Organising a residential that can only be accessed by some students may, in reality, only serve to accentuate differences and works against building a supportive education community. Worst still, it may even establish cliques of 'haves' and 'have-nots'.

Professional expectations and responsibilities of tutors in FE

Wallace succinctly describes a FE professional as someone who has *the ability to recognise, and take responsibility for supporting the rights and needs of learners* (2007, p 67). Students who attend FE have the right to expect that their tutors will do everything possible to ensure their achievement.

Becoming an educational professional and behaving professionally encompasses many features. Although individual tutors will inevitably display degrees of proficiency in each area, a practical interpretation of professional behaviour would include the following.

* *Understanding the role* – Most professional roles have accepted conventions. Before you can be recognised as a professional, you must demonstrate you understand these conventions, know how they should be applied and when to apply them. Usually you will learn these on a training course, such as the PGCE/ProfGCE (Post Graduate Certificate of Education/Professional Graduate Certificate of Education) or CertEd (Certificate of Education). Other behaviours are contextually bound and require you to understand the subtleties of your working environment. You would usually learn these in post.

* *Relevant subject knowledge* – This may seem an obvious statement because of course teachers need appropriate subject knowledge. At the very minimum you should be qualified a level above the level you are teaching. Thus, to teach GCSE (General Certificate of Education) Biology, you should hold at least a level 3 qualification. Interestingly, this minimal approach means many FE tutors will be adequately qualified to teach a wide range of subjects and almost all tutors will be sufficiently qualified to teach basic skills. However, this could be a dangerous assumption as academic qualifications are not a measure of classroom management skills or the ability to motivate students.

* *Classroom management skills* – As a tutor you are expected to be able to effectively manage your class and to promote learning. This is about providing a meaningful role for each of your students and setting standards. The default position must be that every student is in your class to learn, and you are there to teach. The best practitioners will enlist each learner in a collective, collaborative endeavour in which everyone (including you as the tutor) develops their understanding, skills and knowledge.

* *Assessment* – Assessing learner progress is one of your key professional responsibilities. Students need to know the progress they have made and you need to report on their progress. You can only complete this task if you have carried out and recorded regular assessments.

- *Being collegiate* – Teaching is a team effort. You will only become an excellent teacher if you value your colleagues and are prepared to work with them. At the start of your working life you may find you rely far more heavily on your fellow tutors than they rely on you. This is normal. However, as you become more experienced you will be expected to support other colleagues for the mutual benefit of students.

CASE STUDY

Read the case study below about Ruth, and a situation she encountered in her first job in FE.

When I started my first job in FE, teaching was not new to me as I had previously taught in secondary schools. The title of my college job was biology and science tutor. I understood I would be teaching biology A-level and GCSE and providing some science input for other level 2 science courses like BTEC (Business and Technology Education Council), together with being a personal tutor. Overall I had a successful first year. The students I taught achieved well in their year-end exams and I discovered I enjoyed teaching learners in their late teens. I established a good rapport with these students, particularly some of the 'difficult lads' and less able students. In my first year I worked hard to get along with staff and students alike. In fact, at the end of the year I wondered if I had been too willing to please because my head of department, Roy, asked me to take on a pre-GCSE numeracy class. He said it would be a 'new opportunity' and my science background was 'more than adequate for low-level work with numptys'. On one level I could see he needed a teacher for these classes and I was not worried about the academic content as it was well within my abilities. However, at that time I had never taught any number classes, it was outside of my area of experience and I was not offered any additional support to prepare. Looking back, in one respect I was flattered to be asked, but on another level I was really worried I lacked the specialist skills a trained numeracy tutor would have. I was also shocked by his casual dismissal of students as 'numptys'. I was then and am now really resistant to the idea of 'babysitting' classes. I have always believed this to be the antithesis of professional behaviour. I regret not telling Roy about my feelings at the time, but I had only been in the job a year and I did not want to rock the boat.

Critical thinking activity

» *What issues does the case study above raise for you?*

» *How would you have advised Ruth to handle this situation?*

» *What were the potential professional risks for Ruth if she refused to teach the numeracy class?*

» *What were the potential professional benefits for Ruth if she agreed to teach the numeracy class? Are there any caveats Ruth should have considered before agreeing to teach the class?*

» *What were the professional responsibilities of Roy, her line manager, and the college in this situation?*

Discussion: starting teaching

When starting a new role, most staff are keen to fit in as swiftly as possible and recognise they will need the support of their colleagues. Consequently most tutors are willing to co-operate with requests and directions they receive. As Ruth states, she didn't want to 'rock the boat'. However, to be asked to teach outside of your subject discipline is a difficult request.

This request could be interpreted as an endorsement of Ruth's teaching ability, although it may also be a sign of desperation as the college may be unable to find another tutor. Potentially this situation could create real difficulties for Ruth, the students and the college. Teaching is not simply about subject knowledge and there will be a range of subject-specific strategies a non-specialist would not appreciate. While it might be possible to teach a class based on skills developed elsewhere and general understanding, or even charisma, it is not necessarily the best way to teach. Over time this situation could become very stressful and may leave Ruth feeling like an imposter. Ruth is aware of her training need and her line manager should have arranged relevant training to help her take on this 'new opportunity'.

Politically it can be hard to refuse a request from a head of department. However, senior managers have a duty of care towards staff and should not put them in unreasonable situations. Managing this situation would very much depend on Ruth's confidence. Ruth may feel she can say outright she does not feel adequately qualified to teach numeracy. However, she may then fear she will be punished for her decision. Another staff member may try to reach a compromise, for example teaching the group on a six-week trial period or teaching with a support worker in the class. Some staff may involve a third party, like a more experienced tutor, to help reach a resolution. Other staff may accept the challenge of teaching the numeracy group without hesitation. This would be a brave decision and would involve a very steep learning curve.

It is important to remember that ultimately the college has a moral and a contractual responsibility to ensure all learners have a positive and productive learning experience and needs to provide sufficient trained staff to meet this responsibility. Teaching is more than putting bodies in front of classes and students with low skill levels should not be allocated a teacher simply because it is convenient. Nor should such students be referred to as 'numptys'. It is morally wrong that Roy appears to have this attitude. Ruth should seek support from the college's equalities team to help her manage this situation and challenge Roy's behaviour.

Expectations of government agencies and teaching organisations

To a degree, the now dissolved Lifelong Learning UK (LLUK) clarified professional expectations and responsibilities of tutors in FE when it published the *Overarching Professional Standards for Teachers, Tutors and Trainers in the Lifelong Learning Sector* in 2007. When LLUK was dissolved in March 2011, The Learning and Skills Improvement Service

(LSIS) took over the responsibility for setting national occupational standards for all staff in FE. However, the new National Occupational Standards did *not replace or alter national specific standards* released in 2007, rather *they sat above the professional standards … as 'meta-standards'* (LSIS, 2010, p 2). According to the professional standards, FE tutors are expected to *value all learners individually and equally … and … to create effective and stimulating opportunities for learning through high quality teaching* (LLUK, 2007, p 2).

Although lacking statutory powers, the Institute for Learning (IfL), which confers both Qualified Teacher Learning and Skills (QTLS) and Associate Teacher Learning and Skills (ATLS), complemented the standards with its own separate *Code of Professional Practice*. This code identified the values demanded of all FE tutors as:

- *Professional Integrity towards learners, colleagues and institutions;*
- *Respect for learners and colleagues;*
- *Reasonable care to ensure the safety and welfare of learners;*
- *Professional Practice to comply with IfL policy and guidelines;*
- *Disclosure to notify the Institute of any criminal engagement;*
- *Responsibility to comply with the Institute's conditions of membership.*

(Adapted from IfL Code of Professional Practice, 2008, online)

Further, the code specifically emphasised the importance of equality and diversity and required members to

> *act in a manner which recognised diversity as an asset and not to discriminate in respect of race, gender, disability and/or learning difficulty, age, sexual orientation or religion and belief*

(IfL, 2008, online)

This remains a significant statement and clearly signals to FE tutors the importance of diversity and equality.

Teaching unions and professional teaching organisations have no statutory powers in FE. Colleges are not even obliged to recognise these bodies. However, many staff choose to join the largest FE teaching union, the University and College Union (UCU). UCU takes a robust stance on equality and states the union *has a very strong tradition of placing equality at the heart of everything it does [and] challenges discrimination at all levels* (UCU, 2012, p 4). If you join a union, you are expected to follow union rules including taking industrial action.

FE tutors can also join a wide variety of professional organisations such as the British Computing Society (BCS), The British Horse Society (BHS) and the Association for Science Education (ASE). These organisations are concerned with developing the subject expertise of their members. You can join multiple professional organisations in addition to belonging to a single union.

CASE STUDY

Read the case study below which describes Harry's experience of two different conversations.

I do not know what to do or think. I have been spoken to by both the UCU union rep and my line manger today. The UCU rep asked when, not if, I was going to join the union. I said I would think about it. He then, uninvited, proceeded to relate a series of shock stories to me, about a colleague who had been taken to a disciplinary panel for unprofessional behaviour and another tutor who was accused of being a racist by students. I don't know whether he was talking about the work of unions generally or specifically about my college, but he said the union had worked with these people and had helped them to reach a positive outcome. He said what would I do if any of these things happened to me? And on the same day my line manager pulled me to one side to warn me about 'union hot-heads' and how 'if I wanted to get on in college' I shouldn't even 'consider joining a union'. I must have looked a bit bothered, because he said if I had to join a union it should be a no-strike organisation like Voice. I don't know which way to turn.

Critical thinking activity

» *What is your view on teaching and education unions?*

» *What is your view on belonging to a union?*

» *If you chose to join a teaching union would you know whom to contact?*

» *If you have chosen not to join a union do you have other support mechanisms in place?*

» *Where would your priorities be in this situation – to protect yourself from accusations, to show solidarity with colleagues, to secure your personal advancement?*

CASE STUDY

Read the following case study relating to Alan's experience of working with a fellow teacher, Paul.

Paul came to speak with me the other day. We are both fairly new in post and we know each other quite well as we trained together. We have always had a laugh and a joke, and when times were tough we sorted things out by helping each other. I know I would, and I think Paul would too, readily admit we still have a lot to learn. I knew Paul was finding the job difficult, but I was shocked by what he had to say. He said he felt he was not coping; he spent most evenings preparing for classes only to go in and have the work attacked by the students either for being too easy or too hard; he felt his classes were either bored or disruptive; and he was getting to the point where he was dreading coming into work. He was particularly struggling with what he called a 'group of gobby girls'. I had some sort of idea things were not working out for Paul as one these girls had come to see me to ask if she could swap into my class because she thought Paul was a rubbish teacher.

Critical thinking activity

» *What should Alan do in this situation?*

» *What should Alan say to Paul?*

» *Who should be informed of this situation?*

» *Where would your loyalties lie – with Paul, the college, the students or somewhere else?*

Discussion: teaching unions

Unions are an important part of FE. They can help to promote productive and rewarding working relationships to the mutual benefit of the tutor team, college management and students. Some people are nervous about joining a union, viewing them as provocative. Each staff member will have to make their own individual choice in this situation. Before joining any group, tutors should research what the group stands for. Joining a union is a personal decision and it is questionable that a line manager should seek to influence a junior staff member's decision.

It is worth remembering as well as engaging with industrial disputes that unions can represent staff in difficult situations and that membership provides access to a range of useful services including training and, if necessary, legal representation.

Supporting colleagues

In terms of tutor support systems, informal peer support is probably the most common mechanism used by staff. Many problems can disappear after talking them through with colleagues. Paul is struggling in his role. There is good evidence to confirm this: Paul has told Alan that he is having problems and at least one student has tried to swap classes. It is possible Alan may have divided loyalties in this situation, and how Alan responds will be heavily influenced by his personal loyalties.

Informal resolutions can be very useful in tricky situations like this. Alan knows Paul well and is trusted by him. Alan and Paul have worked together for some time and appear to understand each other. In the first instance Alan could consider offering to help Paul with his planning. It seems Paul is pitching the work at the wrong level; if Alan worked with Paul, perhaps they could resolve this problem. This could be beneficial to both Alan and Paul – Paul would gain a solution to his immediate problem and Alan may learn some new ideas. Alan could also offer to carry out an informal observation of Paul. Paul may not be aware of certain issues that would be clear to an outsider. Alternatively, Alan could offer to team teach some sessions with Paul. All of these suggestions would put additional pressure on Alan in the short term, but peer support is based on the simple premise that all members of the education community can seek support from any other member of the community. At some later time Alan may also need support, and having contributed to the community he should feel able to take advantage of the support the community can offer. It is possible, however, that Paul needs other support. He has referred to not coping, and in this instance Paul may need the support of the college counselling services. Alan may need to signpost Paul to these services.

Chapter reflections

This chapter has considered the professional expectations and responsibilities of all tutors in FE. These expectations are formally stated by central government, agencies such as the IfL, and monitored by Ofsted. These expectations are not negotiable and all tutors are expected to achieve minimum standards of behaviour and professionalism. However, all of these standards are on a continuum and different tutors will demonstrate different levels of competence. When you start teaching, your skills level will probably be lower than a tutor who has been teaching for a number of years. This is to be expected. Existing tutors will be aware of this difference as they will remember when they started their careers. Good tutors will want to work with you in your new role and help you develop professionally.

However, new entrants to the profession need to remember they also have skills to offer. New tutors are likely to understand the latest developments in education and are ideally placed to share this knowledge with more established tutors. In this way both new entrants and existing colleagues can develop their skills. There are a number of support mechanisms all tutors can access to ensure their teaching skills remain up to date. These include in-house training opportunities, professional associations and unions. Tutors who are serious about education will seek out development opportunities throughout their working lives so that they can continue to develop and grow professionally.

LEARNING REVIEW AUDIT

Topic	I feel confident in doing this	This is an area I will need to develop
I am aware of the moral argument for implementing robust equality and diversity policies		
I can identify and understand the professional expectations and responsibilities of tutors in FE		
I understand the expectations of government agencies and teaching organisations with regard to tutors in FE		

Taking it further

Lee, J (2012) FE Professionalism Gets Radical Shake-Up. *TES Magazine*, 30 March 2012. Available at www.tes.co.uk/article.aspx?storycode=6202944 Accessed 19 January 2014.

Llukena, A (1998) Qualities and Competencies of the Professional Teacher, *Journal of Educational Reform in Namibia*, 7 (July). Available at www.nied.edu.na/publications/journals/journal7/Journal%207%20Article%206.pdf Accessed 19 January 2014.

www.curee.co.uk Centre for the Use of Research and Evidence in Education

http://plpnetwork.com/ Powerful Learning Practice: Professional Learning

www.theprofessionaleducator.org The Professional Educator

References

IfL, *Code of Professional Practice.* Available at www.ifl.ac.uk Accessed 2 January 2014.

LLUK (2007) *Overarching Professional Standards for Teachers, Tutors and Trainers in the Lifelong Learning Sector*. London: LLUK.

LSIS (2010) *National Occupational Standards for Learning Delivery*. Available at http://repository.excellencegateway.org.uk/fedora/objects/eg:6222/datastreams/DOC/content Accessed 4 January 2014.

Ofsted (2012) *Common Inspection Framework for Further Education and Skills*. Available at www.excellencegateway.org.uk/node/61 Accessed 5 January 2014.

University and College Union (UCU) (2012) *Equality Toolkit*. London: UCU.

Wallace, S (2007) *Teaching, Tutoring and Training in the Lifelong Learning Sector*. Exeter: Learning Matters.

Wedge, P and Prosser, H (1973) *Born to Fail: The National Children's Bureau Report on Striking Differences in the Lives of British Children*. London: Arrow Books Ltd.

3 Race and disability in Further Education: international and national perspectives

Domestic and international responses to disability issues. Inclusive Learning and engaging with diversity

Historical background of race in education. The migration of the race agenda from the US to the UK. Equality, diversity and inclusion of learners

Race and disability in education: international and national perspectives

UK government reaction to increasingly ethnically diverse populations in education. Improving the quality of teaching practice

The politicisation of disability from dependency to entitlement, the evolution of the disability debate. Principles, frameworks and theories which underpin good practice in learning and teaching

Chapter aims

The purpose of this chapter is to help you engage with the evolving race and disability in education debate in the United Kingdom. It begins by considering the historical background of race in education and the migration of this debate from the United States to the United Kingdom. It then considers how the disability agenda has evolved over time and the significance of these developments from an early 'out of sight, out of mind' attitude to a contemporary entitlement approach. You are asked to examine these issues and reflect on how they are relevant to you as a tutor working in Further Education (FE). After reading this chapter and completing the critical thinking tasks you should be able to:

* describe how the race debate moved across the Atlantic from the United States to the United Kingdom;

* identify UK government responses to managing an increasingly ethnically diverse population within education;

* suggest strategies that may be useful within your own workplace when working with diverse ethnic groups;

* identify how you promote inclusion for students with disabilities and additional learning needs in your learning environments;

* engage, with confidence, in discussions about race and disability in education and formulate innovative solutions for meeting the needs of diverse student populations.

Race and education in the United States: a brief history

The first significant numbers of Black Africans arrived in the United States during the 1600s as part of the trans-Atlantic slave trade. Slaves were the property of their masters and while there were some variations in the ways slaves were treated between the different states they lacked any rights, could not own any property of their own or travel away from their master's property unless they had express permission. In many states it was an offence to attempt to educate slaves and consequently most slaves were illiterate and innumerate.

While slavery formally ended on 6 December 1865, equality for Black people was not immediately achieved. In 1896, in a move which supported continued discrimination against Black people, the United States Supreme Court, the highest judicial body in the land sanctioned the separate but equal principle. This principle enabled organisations (including government bodies) and companies to legally segregate races and provide them with separate facilities, *providing* those facilities were of equal standing. Using this principle, the southern states of America kept Black and White people apart in many areas of public life including schools, restrooms and restaurants. While the separate aspect of this legislation was successfully achieved, the equal component was not and Black people were usually given inferior resources such as out-of-date school textbooks and unreliable, overcrowded transport services.

The separate but equal principle was not effectively challenged until the rise of the American civil rights movement when in June 1951, the National Association for the Advancement of Colored People (NAACP) sought an injunction in the US District Court against the Kansas Board of Education, to enable a Black school girl, Linda Brown, to attend her local elementary, White school. However, it was not until May 1954 that the US Supreme Court finally ruled in Brown's favour establishing that racial segregation in schools was unconstitutional and should cease, thus reversing the established separate but equal principle. While the legal argument was won in this landmark case, desegregating US schools took many years to achieve as the court failed to draw up a timetable for implementation of this legislation.

After the Brown ruling, NAACP worked with Black families across America to help them register their children at all White elementary and high schools. With the help of NAACP, nine African-American students registered to study at the all-White Little Rock Central High School, Arkansas. These students were due to start their studies on 4 September 1957 and were intended to be the vanguard of *soldiers in the struggle* (Fordham, 1996, p 62) for a fully integrated education system. However, starting High School for the 'Little Rock Nine', as they were to become known, was not straightforward and became a notorious national and global affair.

The Governor of Arkansas, Orval Faubus, was opposed to integration and ordered the Arkansas National Guard to prevent the Little Rock Nine from entering the school when it opened on 3 September 1957. Faubus was summoned to a meeting by President Eisenhower and instructed to obey the 1954 Supreme Court ruling and allow desegregation to proceed unhindered. Faubus, unhappy with this direction, requested a one-year delay to integrating schools. Eisenhower refused. Undeterred, Faubus used the National Guard to prevent the Little Rock Nine from attending school. Amid growing tension, the Little Rock Nine finally entered the school on 23 September under police escort, only to have to swiftly exit, fearing rioting from a mob of 1000 people who had gathered outside. Angered by these events, Eisenhower issued an emergency directive that all Americans should stop trying to prevent Black students from entering Little Rock High School. On 24 September, Eisenhower took direct action to end the situation, placing the Arkansas National Guard under direct federal control and sending an armoured division of the US army to ensure the continued safety of the Little Rock Nine.

After starting school, the Little Rock Nine endured a year of constant derision, physical and verbal assaults. One of their member, Minnijean Brown, was suspended for retaliating against her White aggressors and in December 1957, after further altercations, she was expelled. She later transferred to a different high school in New York.

In July 1958 Faubus was re-elected as State Governor and in August, still committed to segregation, he passed a law closing all Arkansas state high schools in order to prevent school integration. In September 1958, as a direct result of Faubus' actions, over 3,000 high school students, Black and White, were forced to leave Arkansas in order to continue their education. Finally, after federal intervention in which Faubus' school closure law was identified as unconstitutional, high schools re-opened in August 1959 and small numbers of Black students were admitted to previously all-White schools as part of a controlled integration plan. Fifteen years after the Little Rock Nine originally began their high school education, full integration for all school grades throughout the United States was eventually achieved in

Autumn 1972. However, in some states although taught classes were integrated other extra-curricular activities remained segregated. Indeed Turner County High School in Georgia, another southern state, only organised its first fully integrated prom in 2007 and other high schools in parts of the US still hold separate proms on separate nights for Black and White students (CNN, 2007, online).

Further successful campaigning by the US Civil Rights movement secured the 1964 Civil Rights Act which cemented Black people's right to integrated education, made discrimination in employment illegal, and established a government committee to examine complaints of alleged racial discrimination. Other gains included the 1965 Voting Rights Act which ensured universal voting rights for all US citizens, and in 1967 interracial marriage was legalised in all states. The American civil rights movement also produced a number of prominent leaders including Reverend Jesse Jackson, Malcolm X and Dr Martin Luther King, many of whom travelled to the United Kingdom to seek support for their cause and to publicise events in the United States as well as lending their support to the developing UK civil rights movement.

The separate but equal principle is now a historic artefact prohibited in US law. However, its impact still resonates in American schools. While the 2001 'No Child Left Behind' legislation ensured that *poor and minority children [were] not taught at higher rates than other children by inexperienced, unqualified teachers* (Office of Superintendent of Public Instruction, 2008, p 13), the historic physical and economic separation of Black and White Americans has meant that Black people have had less opportunity to advance and *most African American children … are still denied the education they need to find meaningful and well paying jobs [and] to thrive in college* (ibid, p 6).

Even today, African-Americans still tend to live in poorer districts where there are less well-equipped *low performing schools* (ibid, p 13). More startlingly, attitudes towards African-American achievement seems to have barely shifted from the mentality of the 1800s, when *20 percent [of the population were seen as] leaders, 30 percent as professionals, 30 percent as factory workers, and the last 20 percent as throwaways, generally thought to be incapable of learning* (ibid). African-Americans either as a result of being enslaved or through their contemporary socio-economic location, appear to have been allocated to the 20 percent throwaway population, destined to inhabit the fringes and lower tiers of society. Even more alarmingly in twenty-first-century America, and seemingly at odds with the No Child Left Behind legislation, it appears *almost everywhere, schools have started to re-segregate. Black and White students rarely share classrooms and social segregation is deeply entrenched* (McVeigh, 2004, online).

A further unusual feature of racial segregation in the United States was the development of Historically Black Colleges and Universities (HBCUs), the first of which, Cheyney University, Pennsylvania was established in 1837 for free Black people before the end of slavery by an endowment from Richard Humphreys, a Quaker philanthropist. Although HBCUs are now attended by students of all races, their primary purpose defined by US Congress in the 1965 Higher Education Act was to be a centre of *higher learning whose principal mission was and is the Education of African Americans* (Thurgood Marshall Fund, online). There are 105 HBCUs in the United States today, although a consequence of the 1965 Act meant further HBCUs could not be established.

Critical thinking activity

Take a moment to reflect on the events described above.

» *How aware were you of the situations described?*

» *What relevance does this history have for contemporary US society?*

» *What sort of legacy do you think these events could produce for American society?*

» *What can you identify as further challenges for a fully integrated education system in the United States and what are potential further opportunities?*

» *What parallels can you draw between US and UK education history?*

Race and education in the United Kingdom: a brief history

Records show there has been a continued Black presence in the United Kingdom for nearly 2000 years. Septimius Severus, a Black North African who ruled Britain as a Roman emperor from AD 193–211, ran the empire from here between 208 and 210; and it is possible there were Black people in Britain before this time. Under Roman rule Black people arrived in Britain as enlisted soldiers of *the imperial army* (Fryer, 1984, p 1) and later in the 1500s, *a small group of Africans [were] attached to the court of King James VI of Scotland* (ibid, p 2). However, little is known of Britain's historic Black population and even less is known of the educational fortunes of these Black people. This is because few people outside of the ruling classes, Black and White, received any education until free compulsory schooling was introduced in the United Kingdom for all children aged 5 to 10 in the 1880 Education Act.

Although *African slaves were brought to England from the 1570s onwards* (ibid, p 8) there was no mass resident slave population and in the United Kingdom slaves were either used as fashion accessories for the very wealthy, musicians or sex workers. After the abolition of slavery in the United Kingdom in 1834, Black people in Britain held the same rights as the host White population. However, attitudes developed as a result of Britain's role as a major slave trading nation ensured discrimination towards Black people continued after slavery's abolition.

Critical thinking activity

In 1772, in a landmark legal case which paved the way towards the abolition of slavery in Britain and its colonies, Lord Chief Justice Mansfield is claimed to have stated the air of England is too pure for any slave to breathe and that slavery was so odious that nothing can be suffered to support it.

From this time onwards, slavery in Britain was illegal and resulted in the immediate release of some 14,000 slaves then resident in mainland Britain.

» *How do you think a statement of this nature issued by the Lord Chief Justice would have influenced public opinion in the United Kingdom?*

The impact of colonialism

Because Britain was once an internationally dominant colonial power with an Empire that governed a fifth of the world's population, there has been, and continues to be, regular movement of peoples from all parts of the globe to and from Britain. A further feature of British colonialism was that Britain exported a number of key organisational systems including government, education, defence and civil administration to many different parts of the world. Britain also successfully positioned itself as a global leader in these fields and was, and still is, viewed by many nations as having one of the best education systems in the world. Many people in former British colonies held British passports and had *full participation in citizenship rights in Britain itself* (Rich, 1990, p 149). Consequently, as many nations moved away from colonial rule towards independence a *number of leaders such as Kwame Nkrumah, Jomo Kenyatta, George Padmore and Julius Nyerere* (ibid, p 160), significant African political leaders, chose to complete their education at British universities.

While Britain appeared able to accommodate small numbers of an ex-colonial educational elite, it was not adequately prepared for the mass migration it experienced in the twentieth century when Black people were invited into the country to help rebuild post-war Britain. The *Empire Windrush,* a converted British troopship, brought the first large cohort of colonial migrants to Britain on 22 June 1948, arriving at Tilbury Docks, London (Fryer, 1984). These first travellers were mostly male, having left their families back home in Jamaica. However, later on many were able to either send for their families to join them, or they formed partnerships with UK nationals resulting in a growing population of Black school-aged children attending both primary and secondary schools.

Racial tension in the United Kingdom

Mirroring the challenging events of Arkansas and Little Rock, Britain experienced its own *anti-Black riots in London in 1958* and in Nottingham *there was fighting for 90 minutes between Blacks and Whites* (ibid, p 378). Although there was no official sanction for segregation and while Britain had no history of separate but equal legislation, a widespread informal colour bar existed where Black people were routinely discriminated against in education, employment and housing which the *government and almost everybody else viewed ... with utter complacency* (ibid, p 377).

One of the most startling examples of systematised racism in the United Kingdom was the so-called Boyle's Law which *received official backing from the Department of Education and Science* (Cashmore, 1988, p 40) in 1965. In Southhall, West London, some White parents were worried that the growing numbers of Black and Asian students in local schools were hindering the academic progress of White children and complained directly to the Minister of Education, Edmund Boyle. Boyle responded by *recommend[ing] to government that the proportion of immigrant children should not exceed 30 per cent in any one school* (ibid). This recommendation was accepted and in schools with a population greater than 30 per cent, selected Black students were taken out of school and bused to other schools outside of the district. This practice was adopted by other areas including parts of *Yorkshire, the Midlands and London* (ibid). Busing caused considerable anger in Black communities who had their family lives disrupted as their children were removed from neighbourhood schools, *until it was successfully challenged by the then Race Relations Board in 1968* (ibid). After further campaigning by Black parents and community activists, *by the late 1970s, most authorities which had used busing had dropped the practice* (ibid).

Segregation, stereotyping and schooling

However, the idea of segregated schooling did not fully disappear from all areas and as late as 1987 *26 families in Dewsbury, West Yorkshire, launched a very public protest* (BBC News, 2007, online) regarding the primary school they had been allocated by the local authority, where over 90% of the pupils were Asian. The White parents refused to send their children to their allotted school and opted instead for a *'schoolroom' set up ... in a public house* (ibid) where the children were taught by two retired school teachers. Even by 2007 most *primary schools [had] very little ethnic mix* (ibid) and it appeared that many schools in the area were effectively racially segregated.

Reflecting the challenging race relations in the United Kingdom at the time, in 1971 Coard published his seminal work: *How the West Indian Child Is Made Educationally Sub-Normal in the British School System.* Coard asserted there were

> very large numbers of West Indian children in schools for the Educationally Subnormal, [that] these children [had] been wrongly placed there [and] the authorities [were] doing very little to stop this scandal.
>
> (Coard, 1971, p 5)

Coard highlighted that during the 1960s in the Inner London Education Authority (ILEA) *four out of every five children in ESN schools [were] West Indian* (ibid). As a consequence of Coard's findings, a damning report from the Commission for Racial Equality (CRE, 1974) which claimed too many schools failed to provide an adequate education for Black children and amid growing anger within Black communities, a Government Inquiry chaired initially by Anthony Rampton (1981) and later by Lord Michael Swann (1985) was commissioned to examine the schooling of Black children in the United Kingdom. The final report concluded unequivocally that there was strong evidence demonstrating the academic underachievement of Black students in UK schools and that this underachievement was, in part, caused by *teachers' stereotyped attitudes and negative expectations* (Swann, 1985, p 81). Swann also stated *racism in the education system* (ibid, p 84) contributed to Black students' underachievement.

Following the publication of the Swann report many local authorities took action to try and address inherent failings in the education system, including reviewing the taught curriculum, improving home-school liaison and providing greater in-class support for Black children. These actions, over time, helped to reduce the achievement gap between Black and White students. However, in 2002 Bhattacharyya found:

> approximately a third of Black pupils achieved five or more A*-C GCSEs compared to half of White pupils. In addition, of these Black pupils who achieved 5 or more GCSEs A*-C, about half achieved very high results (8 or more A*-C) compared to two-thirds of all other ethnic groups.
>
> (Bhattacharyya, Ison, Blair, 2003, p 10)

Indeed, later research in 2008–09 by the Department for Children, Schools and Families (DCSF) on the achievement of Black students *has echoed this pattern … replicating previous findings with Black [learners] remaining stubbornly anchored at the very lowest end of achievement* (Peart, 2013, p 21).

Critical thinking activity

Recent research by the DES (Department for Education and Skills) and the DCSF (Department for Children, Schools and Families) confirm that Black students are still one of the lowest achieving groups in education, trailing behind their White counterparts and other ethnic groups. Reflecting on your own workplace:

»   *How well do Black students achieve?*

»   *If there is an achievement gap, what actions have been taken to reduce this gap?*

»   *What further initiatives could be usefully considered?*

»   *How has your organisation linked with other organisations that have successfully supported Black students?*

»   *How has your establishment sought to engage with Black students to gain their views on how well the organisation meets their needs?*

CASE STUDY

In order to try and help Black male students challenge and manage persistent issues of societal and educational disadvantage encountered by many Black people in the United Kingdom today, one college established a Black male student support group. This support group was set up to complement existing college systems and to provide a more appropriate mechanism for meeting the emotional and cultural support needs of Black males. The support group was designed to enable Black males to meet with other *similarly situated people and give them the time … to talk through their everyday life, reflect on that and get ideas from each other* (Morrison, 2008, p 17). In this way the college was able to bring Black male students together and using a structured framework provide opportunities for young Black men to meet and debate issues significant to them. The group was designed to interrupt the usual range of social conversations had by young people and to introduce other topics to challenge their thinking and attitudes. The group followed a planned programme of sessions which included issues such as managing stereotypes of black men; planning for fatherhood; planning their futures; and thinking skills, compulsion and testosterone as well as locally relevant topics such as unemployment. These different areas were intended to help the young Black men develop the necessary skills to manage these issues in a positive way, in an attempt to interrupt a potential cycle of societal disadvantage. These sessions had particular relevance to them as Black men who are often stereotyped as underachieving, irresponsible and feckless.

Discussion: global perspectives on race

Both the United Kingdom and the United States have had a different, but simultaneously startlingly similar, engagement with race in education issues. Neither country can claim a blameless past or to have managed a trouble-free migration into the twenty-first century. Race issues may have evolved and changed, but they still very much remain with both nations as educational achievement statistics organised by ethnic group demonstrate.

And yet progress has been made. In the United States, segregated mainstream education is explicitly outlawed. The overt racism which resulted in so many students losing a year of education in Arkansas is now incomprehensible and it is hard to imagine that any American political figure would be so foolhardy as to carry out such unjust actions. HBCUs, rather than being fringe universities for a minority population, welcome and provide sought-after courses for a diverse range of students. In the United Kingdom, the quaint proclamations of Lord Chief Justice Mansfield sound as an archaic echo of a long forgotten past. Improvements in attainment have been made and while Black students do not achieve in line with their White counterparts, they are no longer the lowest achieving group.

Promoting equality

Significant challenges still remain for both the United Kingdom and the United States. However, many groups both within and outside of education are committed to bringing about positive change for Black and other minority students and ending all forms of racist behaviour and social exclusion. Organisations such as 'Show Racism the Red Card' founded in 1996 as *an anti-racism educational charity* (Show Racism the Red Card, online) provide resources for colleges and schools to challenge the corrosive effects of racism and has made and continues to make a difference to the experiences of Black people in education. Newer campaigns like 'End Racism This Generation' organised by the Runnymede Trust in 2013 is a three-year initiative designed to

> *inspire action to tackle racial inequality, support people to work together in new ways to tackle racism and create lasting solutions to racial injustice so that the next generation will live in a fair, just and equal society.*
>
> (Runneymede Trust, online)

Locally, colleges are setting up their own customised responses to promote achievement and equality, and most colleges now have robust monitoring systems so that it is clear to all college users how well individual groups achieve. Indeed, good practice under the Equalities Act strongly encourages colleges to adopt this approach.

While there is no single solution to fix the inequities of discrimination overnight, progress has been made and organisations like the Runneymede Trust are helping to build on these developments so that we can all play our part in embracing the concept of *Think Global, Act Local* (Geddes, 1915) and make a positive difference for future generations.

UK responses to disability in education: the dependency model

The 1944 Education Act established the system of education we recognise today in the United Kingdom when education was organised *into three progressive stages: primary, secondary and FE* (Fieldhouse, 1998, p 58). Up until this time, scant attention had been given to educating students with disabilities and successive education acts had only focussed on *defective and epileptic children* (Warnock, 1978, p 19). The 1944 Act extended this definition to include *all types of disability* and established *the right to remain in education beyond the age of 16* (ibid) for young people with disabilities. It did not, however, clarify the upper age of entitlement to education. Under the Act, local authorities were required to make suitable provisions for older students with disabilities, although retaining the right to decide how they would meet their obligations towards this group of young people.

While local authorities were encouraged to educate *less seriously handicapped* students in mainstream settings, *those with serious disabilities continued to be educated in special schools* (ibid). Thus, although ostensibly the 1944 Act had a *commitment to equality of opportunity* (Barnes, 1991, p 29) because authorities could choose to educate young people with disabilities separately, it preserved potential inequities within education. Significantly local authorities were also given the power to determine who *required special educational treatment* (Warnock, 1978, p 19), which resulted in considerable regional variation in provision, often causing anger and frustration among disabled people. A further consequence of educating people with disabilities in separate provision was that people in the wider community failed to develop an understanding of the differing needs of disabled people and this gave the impression that *the idea of equality ... did not extend* (Barnes, 1991, p 29) to the disabled community.

In the 1950s attitudes towards people with any kind of disability were firmly rooted in a medical model, where disability was a seen as a deficiency to be fixed and was the sole concern of the person with the disability. At this time there was no concept that society could, through its negative attitudes, be creating barriers to participation. People with disabilities were seen as helpless dependents reliant on the assistance of others, incapable of making decisions and presented as a drain on resources. This is starkly illustrated in Mabel Cooper's story below.

CASE STUDY

Mabel Cooper had learning disabilities and was initially brought up by nuns in secure accommodation with bars on the windows. For the first part of her life she did not attend school at all and could not read or write. In 1952, when she was seven, she moved to secure hospital accommodation, which housed adults and children. Initially she was in a mixed ward with adults, but was then moved to a children's ward where she remained until she was 15. Patients in the hospital were not allowed to wear their own clothes or to have individual possessions and were obliged to follow a strict regimented routine where they were told when to wake, when to go bed and when to eat. Patients were not allowed out of the hospital unescorted to visit the shops on the opposite side of the road. During her time in hospital Mabel recalls that

> *It was just like a prison. You couldn't open the windows, well you could, but not far enough to get out of them. You didn't have toys, no toys whatsoever. There was no school there, they only let you use your hands for making baskets and doing all that sort of thing. In them days they said you wasn't able to learn ... I got used to the hospital. Not really because I wanted to be there, it was because that's what I knew.*

> (Adapted from Cooper, 2003, pp 11–15)

Critical thinking activity

Mabel eventually left hospital care to live as part of the community in supported accommodation.

» *What does this case study tell you about the prevailing attitudes towards people with disabilities?*

» *What are your views on the opportunities provided to Mabel?*

» *How effectively did Mabel's life prepare her for leaving hospital and living in the community?*

» *How does Mabel's experience relate to a contemporary understanding of human rights?*

UK responses to disability in education: towards entitlement

While once disabled people were segregated *from the rest of society* (Brignell, 2010, online) and those labelled as *'feeble-minded'* or *'morally defective'* (ibid) were incarcerated in institutions or hospitals, over time attitudes towards disability have changed. Action by people with disabilities; their families, friends and supporters; disability campaigners; and politicians have all helped to heighten public awareness and understanding of disability issues, creating a broad commitment for the need to *provide a fairer society that would enable each individual to play a full part* (Rose, 2003, p 7). This wider understanding has also been helped by injured military veterans returning from conflict zones and well-known public figures including Stephen Hawking (the world renowned physicist) who has motor neuron disease and Richard Branson (entrepreneur) who has dyslexia, unequivocally demonstrating the contribution that people with disabilities can make to wider society. *Today the emphasis in Britain is on inclusion* (Brignell, 2010, online) and some more politically motivated members of the disabled community *are beginning to proclaim 'Nothing About Us, Without Us'* (Charlton, 2000, p 4). Education has been, and is, at the centre of this driving force for change and greater equality.

The Warnock report

In 1978, Mary Warnock, presented her landmark report on the education of students with special needs which laid the foundations for inclusive education. In it she highlighted the deficiencies of existing education provision and provided a blueprint for a new way of working with students with disabilities. The report began by urging a *more positive approach based on the concept of special educational need* and the removal of the *statutory classification of handicapped pupils* (Warnock, 1978, p 36). Consequently, *the lives and expectations of very many have been transformed* (Tomlinson, 1996, p 3) and students with disabilities now have much greater access to education.

Warnock and FE

With regards to FE, Warnock reminded local authorities the 1944 Education Act required them to *provide for all young people [with special needs] who want continued full-time education between the ages of 16 and 19* (Warnock, 1978, p 171). Unfortunately this duty had rarely been met; and this was presented by Warnock as a wasted opportunity as *for many young people an establishment of further education [would have been] a more appropriate setting … to continue their general education* (ibid, p 173). In order to correct this omission and to make amends for the past, Warnock made a number of specific recommendations for FE including:

- *Wherever possible young people with special educational needs should be given the necessary support to enable them to attend ordinary courses of Further Education;*

- *Some establishments of FE should experiment with modified versions of ordinary Further Education courses for young people with special needs;*

- *Within each region there should be at least one special unit providing special courses for young people with more severe disabilities or difficulties which would be based in an establishment of FE;*

- *Every establishment of FE should designate a member of staff as responsible for the welfare of students with special needs in the college and for briefing other members of staff on their special needs.*

(ibid, pp 351–52)

The Tomlinson report

Building on this foundation, in 1996, Professor John Tomlinson extended Warnock's recommendations and envisaged a FE system which would concentrate on

> *the capacity of the educational system to understand and respond to the individual learner's requirement [and would] move away from labelling the student and towards creating an appropriate educational environment: concentrate on understanding*

better how people learn so that they can better be helped to learn; and see people with disabilities and/or learning difficulties first and foremost as learners.

(Tomlinson, 1996, p 4)

Tomlinson's learner-centred vision for FE required colleges to redesign *the very processes of learning, assessment and organisation so as to fit the objectives and learning styles of the students* (ibid), demanding that teachers *differentiate their approaches according to the previous experience* (ibid, p 5) of their students and recognise the *real difficulties and differences that a disability or learning difficulty can bring into a person's life* (ibid). In Tomlinson's vision FE was not a gift bestowed on some and not others, but was the fulfilment of earlier promises to guarantee students with disabilities equal access to education.

The Lamb report

More recently, FE, recognising that *it is the right of young people to have a say about things that concerns them* (Thomson, 2008, p 1) has begun to engage students with disabilities in making choices about policy that relates to them. The Lamb Report in particular has endorsed the idea of working with wider communities and students to ensure that the needs of disabled people are appropriately met and recommended that learner voice *needs to be strengthened within the system* (Lamb, 2009, p 5). The report further recommended that parents of disabled students *need to be listened to more and brought into partnership with statutory bodies in a more meaningful way* (ibid, p 3). FE has translated these recommendations into practice and student voice should now form *one of the core values underpinning strategic planning and decision-making* (Katsifli and Green, 2010, p 4) in FE. Further, there is *greater emphasis placed on closing the loop between student input and the decisions resulting from that input* (ibid). FE has committed to ensuring that *students with learning disabilities or difficulties ... are enabled to play the same role in student involvement as other students* (ibid) and to be fully engaged in college decision-making processes.

The Equality Act (2010)

All of these recommendations are supported by the 2010 Equality Act, which encompasses all previous equality legislations and *provides a single, consolidated source of discrimination law* (Great Britain, 2013, online) in the United Kingdom. The Equality Act identifies nine protected characteristics including disability, and requires all public sector organisations to:

*   *Eliminate discrimination and other conduct that is prohibited by the Act;*
*   *Advance equality of opportunity between people who share a protected characteristic and people who do not share it;*
*   *Foster good relations across all characteristics between people who share a protected characteristic and people who do not share it;*

(Equality and Human Rights Commission, online)

Significantly, the Act recognises that in the advancement of equality there are times when colleges must *treat a disabled person more favourably than a person who is not disabled to ... ensure that a disabled person can benefit to the same extent [as] a person without that disability* (ibid). This is a dramatic change in legislation as the Act now allows positive discrimination in favour of people with disabilities.

While there is currently both Government endorsement and a legislative framework to promote the rights of students with disabilities, not all colleges have readily embraced the need to meet their obligations and as late as 2010, Ofsted reported that many parents of young people with disabilities still had to *fight for [their] rights* (2010, p 6). Ofsted also reported that:

> *despite extensive statutory guidance, the consistency of the identification of special need varied widely, not only between different local areas but also within them. Children and young people with similar needs were not being treated equitably and appropriately.*
>
> (ibid, p 7)

It appears that for some students in some colleges, equality of provision remains an elusive chimera which is yet to be fulfilled.

Critical thinking activity

» *Having read the different guidance provided by successive Governments, how far does your college comply with the recommendations of Warnock, Tomlinson, Lamb and the legislative requirements of the 2010 Equality Act?*

» *In a recent review of provision for students with special educational needs, Ofsted noted that no one model – such as special schools, full inclusion in mainstream settings, or specialist units co-located with mainstream settings – worked better than any other (2010: 7). What are the implications of this comment for inclusive education? How does this comment articulate with the 2010 Equality Act?*

Responses to disability in education: international perspectives

In 1948, in the aftermath of the Second World War, the 51 member countries of the fledging United Nations (UN) produced the visionary Universal Declaration of Human Rights, thus paving the way for future equality legislation for all nations. Article 26 of this declaration states:

1. *Everyone has the right to education. Education shall be free, at least in the elementary and fundamental stages. Elementary education shall be compulsory. Technical and professional education shall be made generally available and higher education shall be equally accessible on the basis of merit;*

2. *Education shall be directed to the full development of the human personality and to the strengthening of respect for human rights and fundamental freedoms. It shall promote understanding, tolerance and friendship among all nations, racial or religious groups.*

(United Nations, 1948, online)

The UN has continued to be a forward-thinking campaigning organisation promoting co-operation and sharing of good practice between nations for the benefit of all its citizens. Today there are 193 members of the UN, reflecting the truly international nature of this organisation, which remains a powerful international pressure group.

The UN's commitment to securing education for people with disabilities was clearly renewed at the 1994 Salamanca conference when, in collaboration with the Spanish Government and 92 participating nations, it re-asserted

1. *The urgency of providing education for children, youth and adults with special educational needs within the regular education system.*

2. *Education systems should be designed and educational programmes implemented to take into account the wide diversity of needs.*

3. *Those with special educational needs should benefit from a pedagogy capable of meeting their needs.*

4. *An inclusive orientation is the most effective means of combating discriminatory attitudes, creating welcoming communities, building an inclusive society and achieving education for all.*

5. *To adopt as a matter of law the principle of inclusive education.*

(Adapted from the Salamanca Statement, 1994, pp viii–ix)

Although there are ongoing challenges regarding all nations adopting this framework and fulfilling their commitments, under the UN's stewardship there has been significant progress in securing access to education for disabled people. The table below provides examples of the different ways some governments have chosen to implement the Salamanca Statement.

Country	Position
Botswana	As one of the signatories of the 1994 Salamanca statement and the 2006 UN Convention on the Rights of Persons with Disabilities, Botswana *is committed to enhancing education to all her citizens, and inclusive education is perceived to be the most effective way in reaching this goal* (Mukhopadhyay, 2012, online). In furtherance of this goal, Botswana formulated its Revised National Policy on Education (RNPE) which was approved by the national government in 1994. This policy states Botswana will: *[provide] all citizens of Botswana, including those with special educational needs, equality of educational opportunity;*

Country	Position
	prepare [young people] with special educational needs for social integration by integrating them with their peers in ordinary schools; ensure a comprehensive assessment that is based on learning needs which is followed by individualised instruction (ibid). Additionally all education establishments must have a senior teacher who is responsible for special educational needs and leading the institution forward and all teacher training programmes must include information on working with students with special needs.
Canada	In 1982, Canada passed its Charter of Rights and Freedoms. This charter *forms the first part of the Constitution Act of 1982* and *most significantly for persons with disabilities, section 15 ensures 'equal protection and equal benefit of the law'* (McColl et al., 2010, online). According to this charter, *students may not be excluded from the classroom based on any disability. In addition, at the provincial and territorial level there are compulsory education laws supporting the inclusion and accommodation of students with special needs* (Zinga et al., 2005, online). This legislative framework has been a powerful tool in securing mainstream, inclusive education for students with disabilities in all education sectors and in Canada today, *the majority of students are receiving their education in inclusive classrooms in their neighbourhood schools [and] post secondary options have been developed* (Miller, online).
Finland	In Finland, *Finnish sign language is recognised as a mother tongue and students can study with this as their main language* ((Instituto Universitarios de Integracaion en la Comunidad, INICO, 2009, p 100), should they choose to do so, for their entire education career. There are bilingual schools where the language of instruction is both Finnish and Finnish sign language which are attended by both deaf and hearing students.
India	India has adopted a *national action plan for inclusive education* (INICO, 2009:106). To date this action plan has supported the training of *hundreds of teachers; expanded the knowledge base of inclusive education; changed public policy and had a positive impact on public attitudes* (ibid).
Italy	Italy, which has *long been recognised as a leader in creating a national system of inclusive education* (INICO, 2009, p 100), took one of the most progressive positions in relation to inclusive education. In 1971 it passed legislation to *close most special schools and transfer pupils to their local neighbourhood schools* (Mittler, 2000, p 24). At the same time there was a parallel *closure of large psychiatric hospitals and the transfer of mental health services to the community* (ibid, p 25). These reforms meant that students who had been educated separately in discrete provision were suddenly and dramatically integrated into mainstream education. Today *99 per cent of children with special needs are in regular schools and there is still strong support for the principle of integration* (ibid).

Discussion: disability and education

Legislation to challenge disability discrimination was not introduced in the United Kingdom until 1995. This legislation mirrored, to an extent, earlier equality legislation like the 1965 Race Relations Act and the 1975 Sex Discrimination Act. Unfortunately, the 1995 Disability Discrimination Act did not achieve all the disability campaigners had hoped for, but it successfully legislated against the practice of 'out of sight out of mind' and routinely consigning all people with learning and other disabilities to large asylums or hospital accommodation. The Act also recognised the authority and right of people with disabilities to be actively involved in making choices and decisions about their future and relegated the callous treatment of Mabel described earlier to the past.

From a global perspective, initiatives such as the 1994 Salamanca Statement promoted and co-ordinated by the UN have helped to raise the international profile of people with disabilities and to assert their right to be full and included members of every community.

In the United Kingdom, it is not yet clear whether the 2010 Equalities Act will enhance or dilute the rights of people with disabilities. Currently there are no test cases on which to base such a judgement. However, it can be stated that the 2010 Act was designed to enhance and improve the status of all groups who may experience discrimination. Disability rights campaigners will be keen that the Act achieves its goal and that their rights are not eroded in any way.

Chapter reflections

> *If there is one concept that dominates ... social policy discourse in the early years of the twenty-first century it is 'social exclusion'. It is deemed to be the principal reason why contemporary societies lack cohesion. The solution, it is suggested, lies in policies that actively promote social inclusion.*
>
> (Ratcliffe, 2004, p 1)

Schools and colleges are seen as key agents of change in promoting the social cohesion that societies lack; and meeting the needs of ever-increasing diverse populations remains a key objective for all governments. Significant international organisations such as the UN, together with internal national pressure groups, have helped to further the educational equality agenda which has resulted in new laws being passed to guarantee the rights of differing groups. These groups demand that these hard-won rights are respected and met by the education services, and if needed are prepared to challenge the authorities using the legal framework.

Internationally, different countries have interpreted their responsibilities in differing ways. Many countries have tried innovative solutions to their domestic concerns and, through international co-operation, colleges can take advantage of these initiatives. Governments have the opportunity to learn from best practice developed globally and to import ideas from other nations. Not all of these ideas will work and some may require re-interpretation for a particular domestic situation. However, governments can take advantage of ideas that have been trialled elsewhere and can use this knowledge in their efforts to provide the best possible educational experience for minority groups.

LEARNING REVIEW AUDIT

Topic	I feel confident in doing this	This is an area I will need to develop
I have an understanding of significant historical events in relation to race in education		
I feel confident reviewing how my own organisation meets the needs of diverse ethnic groups		
I have a clear understanding of the UK government's expectations of FE in meeting the needs of students with disabilities and additional learning needs		
I understand my individual responsibilities with regard to promoting inclusion for students with disabilities and additional learning needs		

Taking it further

Back, L and Solomos, J (eds) (2009) *Theories of Race and Racism: A Reader.* Abingdon: Routledge.

Benjamin, S (2002) *The Micro-politics of Inclusive Education, An Ethnography.* Buckingham: Open University Press.

Caliendo, S and McIlwain, C D (eds) (2011) *The Routledge Companion to Race and Ethnicity.* Abingdon: Routledge.

Frederickson, N and Cline, T (2007) *Special Educational Needs, Inclusion and Diversity: A Textbook.* Maidenhead: Open University Press.

Gillborn, D (2008) *Racism and Education: Coincidence or Conspiracy.* Abingdon: Routledge.

Lewis, A and Norwich, B (2005) *Special Teaching for Special Children: Pedagogies for Inclusion.* Maidenhead: Open University Press.

www.education.gov.uk/ Department for Education

www.equalityhumanrights.com/ Equality and Human Rights Commission

www.un.org/en/ United Nations homepage

References

Barnes, C (1991) *Disabled People in Britain and Discrimination: A Case for Anti-Discrimination Legislation.* London: Hurst and Co Publishers Ltd.

BBC News (2007) *School Race Row 20 Years on.* Available at http://news.bbc.co.uk/1/hi/education/6998936.stm Accessed 2 August 2013.

Brignell, V (2010) *When the Disabled Were Segregated.* Available at www.newstatesman.com/print/society/2010/12/disabled-children-british Accessed 6 August 2013.

Bhattacharyya, G, Ison, L and Blair, M (2003) *Minority Ethnic Attainment and Participation in Education and Training.* Nottingham: DfES Publications.

Cashmore, E (1988) *Dictionary of Race and Ethnic Relations.* London: Routledge.

Charlton, J I (2000) *Nothing About Us Without Us: Disability, Oppression and Empowerment.* California: University of California Press.

CNN.com (2007) *Students Attend School's First Integrated Prom.* Available at www.edition.cnn.com/2007/US/04/23/turner.prom/ Accessed 3 August 2013.

Coard, B (1971) *How the West Indian Child Is Made Educationally Subnormal in the British School System.* London: New Beacon Books.

Commission for Racial Equality (1974) *Educational Needs of Children from Minority Groups.* London: Commission for Racial Equality.

Cooper, M (2003) Mabel Cooper's Life Story in *Inclusive Education: Diverse Perspectives*, M Nind, J Rix, K Sheehy and K Simmons, London: David Fulton Publishers.

Equality and Human Rights Commission *The Public Sector Equality Duty.* Available at www.equality-humanrights.com/about-us/equality-and-diversity/the-public-sector-equality-duty/ Accessed 8 May 2014.

Fieldhouse, R (1998) *A History of Modern British Adult Education.* Leicester: NIACE.

Fordham, S (1996) *Blacked Out, Dilemmas of Race, Identity and Success at Capital High.* Chicago: University of Chicago Press.

Fryer, P (1984) *Staying Power: The History of Black People in Britain.* London: Pluto Press.

Geddes, P (1915) *Cities in Evolution.* London: Williams and Northgate.

Instituto Universitarios de Integracaion en la Comunidad, INICO (2009) *Better Education for All: A Global Report.* Salamanca: INICO.

Katsifli, D and Green, K (2010) *Making the Most of Student Voice in FE.* London: 157 Group.

Lamb, B (2009) *Lamb Inquiry: Special Educational Needs and Parental Confidence.* Nottingham: DCSF.

McColl, M A, Schaub, M, Sampson, L and Hong, K (2010) *A Canadians with Disabilities Act?* Available at www.69.89.31.83/~disabio5/wp-content/uploads/2011/07/CDA-reformat.pdf Accessed 9 August 2013.

McVeigh, T (2004) *Fifty Years On, Segregation Still Blights US Schools.* Available at www.guardian.co.uk/world/2004/may/09/usa.schoolsworldwide Accessed 29 May 2013.

Miller, B (ND) *Building and Inclusive and Accessible Canada: Inclusive Education.* Available at www.ccdonline.ca/en/socialpolicy/poverty-citizenship/income-security-reform/celebrating-our-accomplishment#sec-incl-miller Accessed 11 August 2013.

Mittler, P (2000) *Working Towards Inclusive Education: Social Contexts*, London: David Fulton Publishers Ltd.

Morrison, N (2008) Ready to Talk. *Times Educational Supplement Magazine*, 9 May.

Mukhopadhyay, H, Nenty, H J and Abosi, O (2012) *Inclusive Education for Learners with Disabilities in Botswana Primary Schools.* Available at Sage Open Online, www.sagepub.com/content/2/2/2158244012451584 Accessed 11 August 2013.

Office of Superintendent of Public Instruction (2008) *A Plan to Close the Achievement Gap for African American Students*. Washington: Office of Superintendent of Public Instruction.

Ofsted (2010) *The Special Educational Needs and Disability Review*. Manchester: Ofsted.

Peart, S (2013) *Making Education Work: How Black Men and Boys Navigate the FE System*. London: Trentham and Institute of Education Press.

Rampton, A (1981) *West Indian Children in Our School: Interim Report of the Committee of Inquiry into the Education of Children from Ethnic Minority Groups*. London: HMSO.

Ratcliffe, P (2004) *'Race', Ethnicity and Difference: Imagining the Inclusive Society*. Maidenhead: Open University Press.

Runneymede Trust (2013) *End Racism This Generation.* Available at www.runneymedetrust.org/projects-and-publications/projects/end-racism-this-generation.html Accessed 17 November 2013.

Rich, P B (1990) *Race and Empire in British Politics*. Cambridge: Cambridge University Press.

Rose, R (2003) Ideology, Reality and Pragmatics: Towards an Informed policy for Inclusion, in Tlisone, C and Rose, R (eds) *Strategies to Promote Inclusive Practice*. London: Routledge-Falmer.

Show Racism the Red Card, *About Our Campaign.* Available at www.srtrc.org/about/about-show-racism-the-red-card Accessed 17 November 2013.

Swann, M (1985) *Education for All: The Report of the Committee of Inquiry into the Education of Children from Ethnic Minority Groups*. London: HMSO.

Thomson, P (2008) Children and Young People: Voices in Visual Research, in Thomson, P (ed) *Doing Visual Research with Children and Young People*. London: Routledge.

Thurgood Marshall Fund *About Historically Black Colleges and Universities (HBCUs)*. Available at www.thurgoodmarshallfund.net/about-tmcf/about-hbcus Accessed 21 July 2013.

Tomlinson, J (1996) *Inclusive Learning: Principles and Recommendations, A Summary of the Findings of the Learning Difficulties and/or Disabilities Committee*. Coventry: FE Funding Council.

United Nations (1948) *The Universal Declarations of Human Rights.* Available at www.un.org/en/documents/udhr/ Accessed 11 August 2013.

Warnock, M (1978) *Special Educational Needs: The Report of the Committee of Inquiry into the Education of Handicapped Children and Young People*. London: HMSO.

Zinga, D, Bennett, S, Good, D and Kumpf, J (2005) Policy and Practice: Acquired Brain Injury in Canadian Educational Systems Education. *Canadian Journal of Educational Administration and Policy*, Issue 43: online. Available at www.umanitoba.ca/publications/cjeap/pdf_files/zinga.pdf Accessed 9 August 2013.

4 Meeting the needs of adult learners

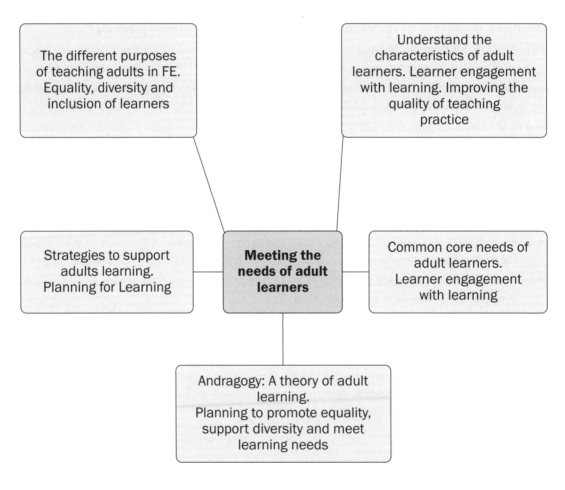

The different purposes of teaching adults in FE. Equality, diversity and inclusion of learners

Understand the characteristics of adult learners. Learner engagement with learning. Improving the quality of teaching practice

Strategies to support adults learning. Planning for Learning

Meeting the needs of adult learners

Common core needs of adult learners. Learner engagement with learning

Andragogy: A theory of adult learning.
Planning to promote equality, support diversity and meet learning needs

Note: Adult is described as any student over the age of 18

Chapter aims

Adult learners form a distinct group within the Further Education (FE) sector. Most adults will have already experienced education in some form at an earlier stage. Many will be re-entering education after a break in learning; some may have only have had the minimal contact with education; and a few may have not been educated in mainstream provision at all. This varied experience produces a distinct set of needs which you, as a tutor, will need to manage.

This chapter considers how the learning environment can be effectively organised to meet the needs of adult students. It considers how some adult learners have to balance and accommodate competing demands such as part-time employment, parenting responsibilities (sometimes as a sole parent) or caring for older relatives, and suggests ways you can meet the needs of all your adult learners.

When you have finished this chapter and completed the critical thinking tasks you will be able to:

*   describe the different and continually evolving purposes of teaching adults in FE;

*   name some of the shared characteristics of diverse groups of adult learners;

*   state a range of common core needs of adult learners;

*   name some of the specific challenges faced by adult learners;

*   describe different strategies to support adults learning in FE;

*   demonstrate an understanding of andragogy and describe this theory's significance for your teaching.

The purpose of teaching adults in FE: an ever-changing context

Adults will have different reasons for choosing to study in FE; *some will want to improve their job prospects, others are looking for intellectual stimulation and others still the chance to make friends or break out of a cycle of isolation* (Stanistreet, 2012, p 9). While the reasons for re-entering education will be different for each student, the purpose of teaching all adults should be identical and is to support each student to achieve *their* identified learning goal, whether this is to gain a GCSE in mathematics, to re-enter employment or to take a more active role in the care of their children. However, FE colleges are not solely concerned with meeting the personal needs and aspirations of individuals and the college curriculum is significantly influenced by contemporary political agendas and priorities. Indeed the political needs of government and increasing globalisation have demanded *an information society ... knowledge economy and ...learning society* (Jarvis, 2010, p 25). FE has been charged with meeting this demand and the oft-vaunted lifelong learning agenda is no longer a luxury but an economic necessity as countries vie with each other to retain or improve their position in a global marketplace. Many more adults can expect to return to education later in life to help them keep up with the changing needs of industry, and recent research by the National Institute for Adult and Continuing Education (NIACE) has shown *adult participation has risen to its highest level in a decade* (Aldridge and Tuckett, 2010, p 9).

One of the first providers of formalised adult education were the Mechanics' Institutes. These were independent organisations established to provide technical education for working adult males. The Institutes received funding from industrialists who wanted a more efficient workforce and philanthropists who were concerned with workers' moral well-being. The first Mechanics' Institute opened in Edinburgh in 1821 and they became so popular that by the *mid-nineteenth century there were 610 Institutes with a membership of more than half a million* (Hyland and Merrill, 2003, p 7). Most FE colleges *have grown from ... the former mechanics' institutes* (Hall, 1994, p 2) and many colleges still continue the tradition of education as a moral social good and for improving work-related skills.

The 1944 Education Act clarified the purpose of FE as providing *full and part-time general education and vocational training as well as (non-vocational) social and recreational education provision* (Frankel and Reeves, 1996, p 7), thus retaining the dual agendas of the Mechanics' Institutes. Over time employers were encouraged to *co-operate with the new colleges ... which gradually became institutions for 'day release' vocational education of the employed or those serving apprenticeships* (Green and Lucas, 2000, p 17) and, at this time, FE was primarily focused on work-specific training.

Meeting the needs of individuals as well as employers

Colleges continued to respond to the needs of industry *reaching a high-point of work-relatedness in the late 1960s and early 1970s* (ibid, p 18). However, during the latter part of the 1970s and early 1980s colleges started to consider the needs of a broader range of clients and were:

> *required to respond to the needs of new types of learners including, notably, adults and school leavers who previously would have directly entered the labour market. Colleges increasingly saw themselves as 'responsive' institutions that not only served the needs of local employers but also the needs of individuals in the wider community, catering for a more diverse student population with a mission of offering a second chance to 16–19 year olds and adults to learn and achieve.*
>
> (Lucas, 2004, p 19)

As the FE target audience grew and diversified, colleges attempted to *cater for everyone, 16–19 year olds, both academic and vocational, adult returners, access students, HE students, those with special needs and those not included anywhere else* (Green and Lucas, 2000, p 35). In 2000, the Department for Education and Employment (DfEE) specifically tasked colleges to:

- *provide higher and improving standards of education for 16–19 year olds. Ensuring increased participation and achievement on broad and balanced programmes of study;*

- *play the leading role in providing the skills the economy needs at craft, technician and equivalent levels through initial technical and vocational education for young people and skills upgrading or re-training for adults;*

- *widen participation in learning, enabling adults to acquire the basic skills they need for employability, effective citizenship and enjoyment of learning;*

- *provide a ladder of opportunity to higher education with a key focus on foundation degrees, built on partnerships with higher education institutions and, with Learndirect, to share and make widely available learning resources.*

(Hyland and Merrill, 2003, p 19)

The Foster review

When the government reviewed FE in 2005, it defined FE's principal purpose as improving *employability and skills in its local area, contributing to economic growth and social cohesion* (Foster, 2005, p 3) once again seemingly shifting the agenda away from self-improvement and towards employment. Although colleges remain obliged to meet this government directive, requiring them to concentrate on the skills needed for employment, most colleges still try to retain opportunities for personal self-improvement.

Critical thinking activity

» *Considering the dual purposes of FE, where do you believe the emphasis currently lies within your own college?*

» *What changes have you witnessed to the curriculum available at your college?*

» *Are you aware of any provision your college no longer offers as a result of changing government agendas?*

» *What is the level of critical debate within your college about the shift in emphasis towards employment and away from the more liberal self-improvement model?*

» *What is your view on these changes and what do you believe should be the primary purpose of colleges?*

» *Considering that some community members may not be able to work as a result of illness or other factors, is it appropriate that colleges should have a lesser emphasis on self-improvement courses?*

» *How inclusive is having a singular focus on employment?*

Characteristics of adult learners

There is no 'typical' adult learner and you will work with many students who have different and varied needs. The diagram on the next page gives some indication of the range of different adult learners you might encounter while teaching and hints at some of the needs you might have to accommodate. However, being an adult suggests other characteristics such as autonomy and a capacity to take personal responsibility for behaviour. While these are

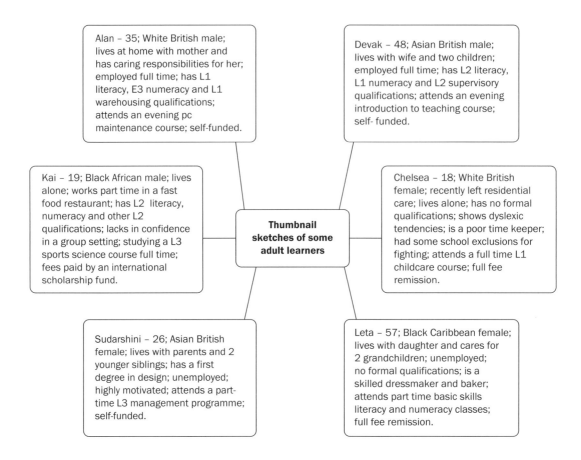

Alan – 35; White British male; lives at home with mother and has caring responsibilities for her; employed full time; has L1 literacy, E3 numeracy and L1 warehousing qualifications; attends an evening pc maintenance course; self-funded.

Devak – 48; Asian British male; lives with wife and two children; employed full time; has L2 literacy, L1 numeracy and L2 supervisory qualifications; attends an evening introduction to teaching course; self- funded.

Kai – 19; Black African male; lives alone; works part time in a fast food restaurant; has L2 literacy, numeracy and other L2 qualifications; lacks in confidence in a group setting; studying a L3 sports science course full time; fees paid by an international scholarship fund.

Thumbnail sketches of some adult learners

Chelsea – 18; White British female; recently left residential care; lives alone; has no formal qualifications; shows dyslexic tendencies; is a poor time keeper; had some school exclusions for fighting; attends a full time L1 childcare course; full fee remission.

Sudarshini – 26; Asian British female; lives with parents and 2 younger siblings; has a first degree in design; unemployed; highly motivated; attends a part-time L3 management programme; self-funded.

Leta – 57; Black Caribbean female; lives with daughter and cares for 2 grandchildren; unemployed; no formal qualifications; is a skilled dressmaker and baker; attends part time basic skills literacy and numeracy classes; full fee remission.

desirable adult characteristics you will work with adults who, for a variety of reasons, will not demonstrate these characteristics.

While you can expect the adults you teach to have different life experiences and levels of understanding they will all share some common unifying characteristics which are relevant for their learning and for your teaching. These shared characteristics include the following.

- *Previous Experience* – Adults bring years of experience, from education, work and life to college. One of the difficulties you may encounter is that adult students sometimes do not value the knowledge they have developed outside of formalised education settings and fail to see its relevance for learning. The challenge for you is to demonstrate to students how learning which happens in non-formal settings can be useful in college and how, as a consequence of practical experience, they could be an expert in a particular field. For example Devak, as a result of his supervisory work, may be able to bring classroom management skills to the teacher training course.

- *Expectations – Adults expect to be taught and expect to learn* (Reece and Walker, 2004, p 7). Many adults studying in FE will have completed an extended, and possibly painful, decision-making process before deciding to commit to further study. Once they arrive in FE they do not expect to have their time wasted. As their tutor you need to acknowledge and respect their desire to be taught and ensure that you provide relevant learning opportunities.

- *Existing knowledge* – Some adult learners may challenge your knowledge and advise you that they were not taught certain facts. If adults are relying on inaccurate data, you will need to correct their misunderstandings. For example, if some of your adult students state that there were no Asian soldiers in the First World War, you will need to inform them that this is wrong and the Gurkhas and other Asian soldiers fought in both the First and Second World Wars.

- *Existing patterns of behaviour or fixed belief systems* – A popular and unflattering adage states that *you cannot teach an old dog new tricks.* However, as an adult educator, this is an inherent part of your role and you are obliged to help adult students learn new ways of working and being. If an older learner refers to Black people as 'coloured' and women as 'ladies', while they may not be intending any offence, this is outdated terminology. You are again obliged to identify this issue for all students in your class. This is important for everyone's learning: to show respect to the group being described, even if you do not have any of that particular group in your class; and to ensure that you are meeting the requirements of the 2010 Equalities Act which requires you to challenge discriminatory behaviour and to advance positive relations between different groups. Equally, methods of teaching have changed and some older learners may feel uncomfortable with being asked to contribute to discussions or to engage in the co-construction of knowledge. This may be because when they attended school the only legitimate voice in a learning environment was that of the teacher's and students' views were not valued. You will need to work with these learners to demonstrate that you respect their views and that you want to hear what they have to say.

While the above features of adult behaviour may be potentially challenging, adult learners also display many positive characteristics which aid learning, including the following.

- *Independence* – One of the features which separate adult learners from younger students is that they will all have learnt different strategies to help them manage their everyday responsibilities. How successful or appropriate these strategies have been may be debatable; however, they will all have some coping skills and many adults prefer to manage their own affairs rather than be closely directed. Additionally, most adults, even if reluctantly, will take responsibility for their actions. Independence and personal responsibility are key characteristics of successful learners. You will need to harness these strengths and work with your students so that they can apply them within the learning environment.

- *Maturity* – Parents and carers, in frustration, often exhort their children to 'grow up' or to 'act their age'. Most adults will have grown up and will appreciate commonly accepted boundaries of responsibility. This will mean they already understand the need to attend sessions punctually, bring appropriate equipment, it is impolite to interrupt someone who is talking and the need to organise themselves and their workloads. These are positive pro-study behaviours and will support achievement in college.

- *Motivation* – Many adults have chosen to return to learning not because they have been instructed to or because they are required to, but because they want to. However when they arrive in college they expect the work to be relevant as many, especially if they are studying a vocational course, will want *to implement their learning immediately* (Rogers, 2002, p 75). While implementing learning may mean your students are not yet experts in a particular skill, the fact that they are applying their learning will help them to make swifter progress when they are back in college.

Critical thinking activity

»   *Considering the six thumbnail sketches provided earlier, what additional skills can you identify these students might have which they could bring to the learning environment?*

»   *What sort of support needs, if any, do you envisage these students may have?*

»   *How do you think this could impact on the students' learning?*

»   *Would your college be able to provide appropriate learning support?*

»   *Would you be responsible for providing this support directly or would this support be offered in some other way?*

»   *What are the centralised student support facilities in your college?*

»   *What is the process for requesting learning support from central services?*

»   *What is your role in working with students who need additional support?*

»   *Is the support provided by your college time limited or are there any other restrictions you are aware of that could limit any support provided?*

CASE STUDY

Barry is a 45-year old White UK national who has joined your part-time introduction to teaching course. On successful completion of this course Barry would meet the minimum recognised threshold to teach in a college. He was a keen sports person in his youth and played full time as a professional in a lower division team. However, an early injury forced him to retire and he re-trained as a printer and he now works full time in this industry. He maintained his interest in football and voluntarily coached youth teams in his spare time. Barry believes it is his past experience which earned some of these teams promotion to higher divisions. He enjoys working with young players and it is now his ambition to use his footballing skills to gain a teaching post in a college.

You observe that in group exercises, Barry has a tendency to dominate discussions and appears reluctant to allow others to contribute. When others are speaking you have noticed that Barry interrupts them to explain how he would approach a particular situation. Some of the group seem wary of Barry and appear hesitant when asked to work in a group with him. At the end of one of your sessions when you had talked about political influences on the funding of education you overheard Barry say that he *didn't understand what politics had to do with education,* he *hadn't come on the course for a political lecture* and that he *just wanted to teach boys football.*

Critical thinking activity

» What issues does the situation described raise for you?

» What skills can you identify that Barry has? How might these be useful in a teaching situation?

» What development points can you identify for Barry?

» What are your responsibilities towards Barry?

» What are your responsibilities towards the rest of the group?

» How would you prioritise these different responsibilities?

» What are the implications of Barry's continued presence for group cohesion?

» How would you choose to manage this situation?

» If another group member complained directly to you about Barry and stated they would leave if Barry stayed, how might this influence your response?

Discussion: the purpose of FE

FE has a long and proud history. While there may be tensions between liberal self-improvement and instrumentalist work-focused agendas, FE has always retained its ambition to provide a meaningful, useful education experience for all its students. To this end, it has endeavoured to have a broad curriculum that appeals to the diverse needs of students and employers. However, it has also witnessed repeated funding changes and it has been obliged to redesign its curriculum again and again, sometimes resulting in whole programmes being removed from the curriculum. These externally imposed changes have often been introduced suddenly and dramatically and many colleges have had to respond swiftly, simply to survive. This need for expediency has forced many tutors to focus on the immediate, leaving no time for critical debate or discussion on the purpose of education.

The thumbnail sketches provided earlier in this chapter could never represent the full diversity of students and while it is a tall order to ask lecturers to be *all things to all people*, as a tutor it is your professional responsibility to at least have an awareness of the range of needs in your college as a whole and how these may be supported. If you cannot meet a student's need, you should understand what internal and external services exist and how you would request this support.

External influences on tutors

Barry, as a trainee tutor, has some defence for not fully appreciating how education has become politicised. You, however, should not be demonstrating such political naivety. Indeed you have a responsibility to educate Barry about the wider influences on education and how these impact on his teaching. Although this may be challenging and not an area Barry wishes to engage with, he needs to realise that he does not teach in a vacuum. In the situation described it would be useful to have an individual tutorial with Barry where you address his political reluctance and advise him of the impact his behaviour is having on the rest of the group. It is possible he is genuinely unaware of the tensions in the group and could be surprised to learn of the difficulties he is creating. Equally, there is a chance he may not accept your advice, in which case you would need to firmly and clearly remind him of the group ground rules and the need to value the contributions of others. You will also need to find the time to speak to the student who threatened to leave the course and assure them you are dealing with the situation.

Needs of adult learners and strategies to support adults' learning

Before deciding to embark on a course, many adults will have debated their choice for a considerable time and may be anxious about beginning study. It is your responsibility to ease their transition into learning and to make their time at college both enjoyable and profitable. In the same way that there is no typical adult learner, there is no teaching blueprint that will guarantee success for all adults. However, when teaching adult students it is good practice to apply the following principles.

- *Show respect to 'all' adult learners* – This is absolutely critical and you need to ensure you always treat adult learners fairly and respectfully. This is not the same as accepting everything that adult students say or do and you must be prepared to challenge discriminatory or unacceptable practices. While you may disagree with a student's opinion, you must still be prepared to listen to and work with each student. Take care to avoid indiscreet behaviour such as discussing students' ages and demonstrate you value adult learners as equals. At all times avoid patronising mannerisms or belittling behaviours. This includes ensuring you pronounce students' names correctly; understanding that older learners have different interests and may not wish to discuss contemporary street fashions; and acknowledging some adults still hold certain values such as deference for authority figures. Depending on the learning situation you may wish to consider opening a wider discussion on why and how these values have changed over time.

- *Adopt a flexible approach to accommodate complicated life styles* – Many adults are *faced with multiple, often competing demands from work, education, family and leisure* (Dzubinski et al., 2012, p 103). They may be caring for children or older relatives; experiencing the challenges of pregnancy and becoming parent; or learning to cope with a bereavement alongside work and other commitments. While these are not exclusively a condition of adulthood, because of the nature of these events, it is likely that more adults will experience these situations than younger students. These events are both emotionally and practically challenging and may result in adults giving less attention to their studies. Although colleges have to set parameters of expected behaviour, these parameters need to be applied with understanding and should accommodate individual student needs while helping them achieve their learning goals. If your college adopts a very strict attitude towards applying college policies which do not appear to cater for difficult situations, you may need to refer some cases to your line manager so that they can adjudicate on particularly difficult situations.

* *Provide regular feedback to help direct student development and understanding* – Adults are often clear on their reasons for studying and need feedback to inform them of their progress. Less confident adults may also need reassurance that they are achieving expected levels. You need to provide your adult students with timely and well-structured feedback so that they can self-assess their own progress. This will help adult learners to identify their personal development areas and will support them to engage in a productive learning dialogue with you about their work.

* *Support your students to use new learning technologies* – The twentieth and the twenty-first centuries have witnessed phenomenal changes in the pace of technological change. Some adult learners, particularly if they have been away from learning for some time, may be bewildered by the changes in education. E-learning is no longer peripheral to education but occupies centre stage with students being directed to participate in blogs, e-conferences, wikis and to make use of mobile and other new learning technologies. You have two-fold responsibilities here. Firstly you need to ensure that you are attending to your own training needs and are keeping pace with developments so you can integrate new technologies into your teaching and ensure your learners are not disadvantaged; secondly you need to introduce new technologies in a way that supports learning rather than confounds and frustrates learners. It may be useful to adopt a staged approach or to pair adult learners with students who are more familiar with using e-learning.

* *Create a community of learners to which they belong* – Adult learners *feel the need to build learning communities* (Dzubinski et al., 2012, p 106). As a tutor, this is your responsibility. You need to engender a spirit of belonging and group cohesion so that students will want to attend sessions, feel inspired to return and are willing to share ideas with each another. One strategy to help achieve this is to establish communities of practice. These can be set up for the academic year or could be rotating and task focused. Depending on the nature of the group you could choose to ask your students to set these groups up. However, this may be a risky strategy and you would have no control over whether the groups would be organised in a useful way or could simply become gossip clubs. A potential compromise is initially to organise the groups yourself, having due regard to group dynamics and levels of understanding, and set times for the groups to meet. At this stage it would be helpful to provide an agenda for the group to focus their attentions and direct their actions. Later, when the groups have become more settled you could hand over responsibility to students to organise their own schedule of meetings.

Andragogy: a theory of adult learning

Andragogy, a theory which describes how adults learn and best practice in teaching them, was developed by Malcolm Knowles *in the early 1970s* (Knowles et al., 2011, p 1) in the United States. Until Knowles advanced his theory, pedagogy – *the art and science of teaching children* (Knowles, 1983: 53) – had dominated thinking on learning and teaching. Unfortunately, many teachers continue to teach adult learners *as if they were children* (ibid) and fail to recognise the distinctive needs of adult students. This is both disrespectful and ill-advised. Many adults will, with due cause, resent being treated as a child and this will have a negative impact on your relationship with students, preventing you from helping adult students to achieve their full potential.

Knowles argued that adults learn differently from children, and that tutors of adults need to take into account the way adults' life experiences influence their learning. He set out six core *alternative ... assumptions* (Knowles et al., 2011, p 71) which he believed should underpin all adult teaching. He identified these as:

1. the need to know: adults need to know why or how knowledge will be useful;

2. self-concept of being: adult learners have an understanding of their own being and can self-direct their learning;

3. prior experience of the learner: learners will bring a range of education and life experiences with them to learning;

4. readiness to learn: adults engage in learning if it will increase their capacity to cope with other demands;

5. orientation to learning; adults are life and problem centred and are more likely to participate in learning if it supports them in their daily lives; and

6. motivation to learn: learners have identified personal reasons to engage with learning.

(Adapted from Knowles et al., 2011, p 3)

Although you may not feel all adult students have developed all these characteristics, you still need to adopt Knowles' framework of assumptions in order to demonstrate you value and respect the adult learners in your classes and acknowledge them as equals.

CASE STUDY

During one of your teaching sessions you have observed that one of the three older students in a mixed age-range class appeared frustrated and angry at times. The older student did not voice any comments during the course of the lesson but you decided to speak to him individually at the end of the session. During your conversation he informed you that he *had come to college to learn* and did not realise he *would be in a kindergarten class, with idiots who just wanted to text on their mobiles*. He further informs you that as a self-funded student he does not have *time or money to waste*, expects to have the opportunity to learn and that as a tutor you should be helping him to do this.

Critical thinking activity

»   *What issues does this situation present?*

»   *How would you choose to manage this situation?*

»   *What action needs to be taken to promote greater group cohesion?*

»   *How can you support adult learners effectively in a mixed age-range group?*

»   *How would you manage this student's derisory comments about younger learners? What would you want to say to the group, if anything, about the adult student's apparent frustrations?*

»   *Would you consider giving the adult student independent work they can complete in the library away from the main cohort?*

Discussion: challenging student behaviour

Students choose their courses. They do not choose their tutors or the other students in their classes. While students are part of the college and class community, they do not manage the learning process. This is your job as a tutor. In the situation described you need to work to ensure all students respect each other and ideally are happy to work with each other. It is not helpful to refer to other students as idiots. You need to inform the older student that you expect him to show the respect that he requires of others and ask that he allows you the opportunity to address the situation. You need to engineer ways of having different students work together. This could include setting random or purposely selected groups. You will also need to address the texting issue. If this behaviour is against agreed ground rules, you need to challenge the students. Depending on the frequency and nature of the texting you might consider setting up a 'phone-box' for students to deposit their mobiles in at the start of the class. However, you should only consider an action like this if you are very concerned or have agreed a 'no phones' ground rule with your students or if there is a 'no phones in class-room policy' at the college, as it could be seen as contrary to the philosophy of FE according to which you are expected to value your students as responsible, autonomous adults. You would also need to be confident that you could guarantee the safe return of all mobiles to their owners. And it is not a solution to give the adult who complained independent work in the library. This would just be a short-term containment strategy and runs the risk that the adult may feel isolated and victimised.

Chapter reflections

Adults make up the majority of the student population in FE. However, they sometimes seem to be an almost a forgotten population and colleges are more concerned with focusing on the needs of their full-time 14–19 students. Adults, as a consequence of their age and because of the different coping strategies they have developed are often assumed to be self-supporting learners who do not require assistance in their learning. It is your responsibility to be alert to the general learning needs of adult students and also to be aware of the specific learning needs of the adult students in your group. This is your first challenge as a tutor of adults and you need to appreciate that motivating people to learn new skills – particularly when their experience of education has been negative – will depend first on nurturing their identity as capable learners (Crowther, 2011, p 15).

Although many adults may be competent, independent individuals capable of organising themselves, it is unreasonable to assume that all adults will have developed the skills to be successful learners. Indeed because adults are older learners they will have different learning needs to younger students and they may be feeling nervous about returning to learning. You will need to support them in this transition and to create a climate which enables them to feel a valued member of the college community, confident to make contributions. You will also need to manage the different expectations of adult and younger learners so that each member of the group feels respected.

LEARNING REVIEW AUDIT

Topic	I feel confident in doing this	This is an area I will need to develop
I can identify the different purposes of teaching adults in FE		
I have an understanding of the characteristics of adult learners		
I am aware of the common needs of adult learners		
I can identify strategies which would be useful to support adults learning		
I have an understanding of andragogy and appreciate its relevance to my teaching		

Taking it further

Petty, G (2004) *Teaching Today, A Practical Guide*. Cheltenham: Nelson Thornes.

Rogers, A (2003) *What Is the Difference, A New Critique of Adult Learning and Teaching*. Leicester: NIACE Publications.

Scruton, J and Ferguson, B (2014) *Teaching and Supporting Adult Learners*. Northwich: Critical Publishing.

Sutherland, P (1998) *Adult Learning, A Reader*. London: Kogan Page.

www.naice.org.uk National Institution for Adult and Continuing Education, Leicester

References

Aldridge, F and Tuckett, A (2010) Change for the Better. *Adults Learning*, May 2010.

Crowther, J (2011) Too Narrow a Vision. *Adults Learning*, Winter, 2011.

Dzubinski, L, Hentz, B, Davis, K and Nicolaides, A (2012) Envisioning an Adult Learning Graduate Program for the Early 21st Century. *Adult Learning*, 23(3): 103–10.

Foster, A (2005) *Realising the Potential: A Review of the Future Role of FE Colleges*. Nottingham: DfES.

Frankel, A and Reeves, F (1996) *The Further Education Curriculum in England, An Introduction*. Bilston: Bilston College Publications.

Green, A and Lucas, N (2000) *FE and Lifelong Learning: Realigning the Sector for the Twenty-First Century*. London: Institute of Education.

Hall, V (1994) *Further Education in the United Kingdom*. London: Collins Educational.

Hyland, T and Merril, B (2003) *The Changing Face of Further Education*. London: RoutledgeFalmer.

Jarvis, P (2010) *Adult Education and Lifelong Learning: Theory and Practice*. London: Routledge.

Knowles, M S (1983) Andragogy: An Emerging Technology for Adult Learning, in Tight, M (ed) *Adult Learning and Education*. London: Croom-Helm.

Knowles, M S, Holton, E F and Swanson, R A (2011) *The Adult Learner*. Oxford: Butterworth-Heinemann.

Lucas, N (2004) *Teaching in Further Education* London: Institute of Education.

Reece, I and Walker, S (2004) *Teaching, Training and Learning, A Practical Guide*. Sunderland: Business Education Publishers Limited.

Rogers, A (2002) *Teaching Adults*. Maidenhead: Open University Press.

Rogers, J (2003) *Adults Learning*. Maidenhead: Open University Press.

Stanistreet, P (2012) Still Learning After All These Years. *Adults Learning*, Summer: 8–11.

5 Working with younger learners and the impact of youth on learning

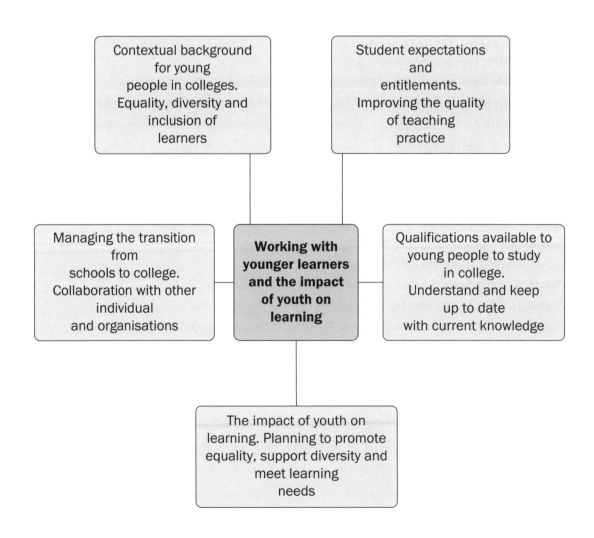

Contextual background for young people in colleges. Equality, diversity and inclusion of learners

Student expectations and entitlements. Improving the quality of teaching practice

Managing the transition from schools to college. Collaboration with other individual and organisations

Working with younger learners and the impact of youth on learning

Qualifications available to young people to study in college. Understand and keep up to date with current knowledge

The impact of youth on learning. Planning to promote equality, support diversity and meet learning needs

In this chapter, *younger learners* is used to describe any student studying in college under the age of 16, *young learners* is used to describe students aged from 16–18, and *adult learners* describes all those students who are older than 18. *Young people* will be used in a generic way to describe all students aged 14–19.

Chapter aims

While many young people understand what it means to be a pupil in school they have yet to learn what it means to be a student in college. This chapter explores the implications of this transition for students and tutors. By the end of this chapter you will be able to:

*   describe the historical background for young people studying in college;

*   recognise the challenges that young people face moving from mainstream schools to college;

*   list helpful strategies to use in supporting young people to make the transition from school to college;

*   identify the range of qualifications available for young people to study in college;

*   describe the different attendance patterns available to young people studying in college.

Young and younger learners in colleges: a contextual background

The education and purposeful engagement of pupils who have finished their primary education has long occupied the thoughts of educators, policy makers and politicians. As early as 1927, the Board of Education mapped out its ideas for educating students after their primary schooling, when it proposed

> *providing a universal system of post-primary education ... for all normal children between the ages of 11 and 14, and, as soon as possible 11 and 15 ... which will generally be controlled by the common aim of providing for the needs of children who are entering and passing through the stage of adolescence.*

> (Hadow Report, 1927, pp 172–73)

To achieve this aim the government established different kinds of provision matched against the perceived differing abilities and aptitudes of young people. The most academically able students were to attend grammar schools and be taught a *predominantly literary or scientific curriculum* (ibid, p 175), while those who would exit education straight into employment would receive a more *'realistic' or practical curriculum* (ibid) in modern schools.

Interestingly, even in the 1920s, the government also suggested that state education should be underpinned by *humane or liberal* (ibid, p 174) principles and was a means of developing the whole person, not simply equipping individuals to enter industry. This principled position echoed the cherished FE notion of andragogy where contributions from students are encouraged in a *relationship of mutual respect between teacher and learner* (Vella, 1994, p 182) and the *tutor honours the learner first as an adult with years of experience* (ibid, p 185). Equally interestingly while encouraging reciprocal respect, the government also endorsed the use of corporal punishment as a legitimate means of enforcing discipline, a system which was only formally abolished in English state schools in 1987 and independent schools in 1998.

Although FE now forms part of mainstream education it did not exist in the first half of the twentieth century and *did not enter the educational lexicon* (Hyland and Merrill, 2003, p 6) until 1944 when *it was used to refer to post-school provision in section 41 of the 1944 Education Act'* (ibid). The 1944 Act also laid the foundations for the post-war and successive governments *to build the present FE system* (Lucas, 2004, p 13) by enabling Local Education Authorities (LEAs) to *establish and maintain county colleges, which provided school leavers with vocational, physical and practical training* (ibid, p 14) for learners who had concluded compulsory schooling and adults in employment. These two groups of students remained FE's principal market until very recently.

While small numbers of younger learners may have occasionally attended FE on a part-time basis since about the 1970s to study subjects not available in schools, very few students under the age of 16 made this choice. However, this situation changed suddenly and significantly in 2002 when the Increased Flexibility Programme (IFP) was introduced. As part of this initiative, secondary schools were able to form collaborative arrangements with colleges to provide a *more diverse curriculum* (Ofsted, 2005, p 2) and *vocational learning for 14 to 16 year olds* (ibid, p 1) for whom the traditional curriculum was inappropriate. The IFP allowed younger students to attend FE colleges for part of the week to study *National Vocational Qualifications (NVQs) or other vocational qualifications* (Ofsted, 2005, p 2) while still administratively enrolled at school. Under this scheme, younger learners have attended colleges to study many different courses such as painting and decorating, hair and beauty and motor vehicle maintenance.

Because of the success of the IFP where pupils *gained more points than might have been expected given their prior attainment and other background characteristics'* (Golden et al., 2005, p 35) and made better than anticipated progress this programme has been retained. Colleges can now realistically expect the numbers of younger learners studying in colleges to increase. Indeed the numbers of 16 to 18 year-olds studying in colleges is also likely to increase as recent changes in legislation now mean *all young people in England must continue in education or training until … they turn 17 from 2013 and until their 18th birthday from 2015* (DfE, online). As a tutor you need to be aware of the impact of these changes and will need to consider how you will manage these increased populations of young people, some of whom may be studying in the same class as adult learners.

Managing the school–college transition

Leaving school is a challenge that, at some time, all young people will face as they exit either into employment, a training post or to another form of education. While some young people will have begun their college career at 14 through the IFP, many more young people enter college at 16 to continue their education. Moving to a college environment is a significant event for both 14–16 year olds and over 16s as they exchange familiar surroundings for a new environment and many students, especially younger students, require support in managing this transition.

Strategies to support a successful transition

Both colleges and schools have a responsibility to establish processes that support the successful transition of young people to college and to promote their swift integration into college life. The arrangements for supporting 14–16 year olds who attend on a part-time basis and 16 year-old students who may be attending on a full-time basis will necessarily be different.

Useful strategies to support 14–16 year olds may include the following.

- *Identifying college and school staff responsible for supporting students* – It is good practice for colleges engaged with the IFP to identify named college staff responsible for the daily pastoral care of school students in college. This may be the college tutor who teaches the group, or it could be a separate dedicated team of pastoral support staff. The name(s) of college staff should be clearly and openly communicated to the school, the students and possibly to the students' parents/carers. The school should also inform the college of a named school contact who is responsible for managing IFP students when they are in college. It is important that school staff share relevant records with college staff so that the college is in the best position to support new intakes.

- *Arranging taster sessions* – IFP students could be invited to attend college taster sessions. The function of such sessions is to allow students to become familiar with the college premises, to meet key college staff (this would include their course tutor and may include a member of the college senior team) and be introduced to the sort of work they would study at college. Students could also be informed of college rules and any equipment they would need to bring to college. If the school and college agreed, taster sessions could also involve inviting parents or carers to attend.

- *Providing college information packs* – School students and their families may be unfamiliar with the expectations of college. It is helpful to provide an information pack which includes basic information such as the contact name of the college tutor; the address of the college site the student will attend; college telephone or email contact details; details of public transport to travel to college if necessary; details of dress code while at college; timetable details and information on any essential equipment needed. Site maps with key areas students will use are also useful.

- *Establishing a buddy system* – Some school pupils may feel particularly vulnerable when studying at college. For these students it may be useful to have a college buddy to help them adjust to college. Buddies could take responsibility for meeting school students when they arrive at college and be with them during break or social times. This role could only be allocated to more responsible college students and would need to be compatible with existing college students' study or other commitments. It is likely that this would be a time-constrained arrangement as the school students acclimatise to college life.

- *Having a safe zone* – This could be used in conjunction with a buddy system or could be used instead of a buddy system. The safe zone would be used as an area for school students to socialise away from other college social zones used by older students in break periods. Should any difficult situations arise it is useful to inform students of support services such as counselling.

Strategies that are useful in supporting 16 year olds when they join college for the first time include the following.

- *Provide a well-structured induction programme* – Students joining the college for the very first time may have similar fears and anxieties to 14 year olds starting college. For these students it may be useful to have an extended induction programme. This may mean starting term earlier by anything from a single day to a week, to allow these students a chance to become familiar with their new surroundings before the majority of the students begin. This offer would be a voluntary opportunity for students and it is unlikely that it would be needed for older students or more confident 16 year olds. The induction programme allows students to receive their course timetable; meet other students on their course; meet college staff; be advised of college rules and regulations; complete enrolments if necessary; be given essential documentation such as college identity badges and/or library cards.

- *Allocate each student a personal tutor* – A personal tutor is responsible for pastoral care of a group of students and acts as a central contact point for questions about all college business. Personal tutors provide essential information, help students settle into college life and help to resolve any problems or difficulties students are experiencing.

- *Signpost students to information points* – Colleges are large complex organisations. They often have other departments students need to access which could include finance offices, counselling services, health services, family planning services or accommodation centres. Alternatively, some colleges now offer many of these support facilities online or have adopted centralised 'one-stop' information points. These information points allow students to collect information they need from one single point, removing the need to visit multiple offices or sites. Students need to be advised where to find these information points so they can access services when or if they need them.

Building relationships and maintaining professional boundaries

Students are in college to learn. It is therefore important that they are given the chance to learn and that as a tutor you do not label students *as evil, unteachable or thick* (Haydn, 2012, p 106). Such negative attitudes make it difficult to teach students and to support them to succeed. It is even more critical to build appropriate professional relationships with younger students who may have to simultaneously accommodate both school and college rules. It is particularly important for younger learners to avoid any potential confusion or contradiction between these two sets of rules.

Building successful relationships begins with values and teaching in FE *is underpinned by a set of professional values that should be observed by all teachers, tutors and trainers in all settings* (LLUK, 2007, p 3). The very first value identified in the *New Overarching Professional Standards for Teachers, Tutors and Trainers in the Lifelong Learning Sector* clearly states the *lifelong learning sector values all learners, their progress and development, their learning goals and aspirations and the experience they bring to education* (ibid). Although these values and standards are to be *reviewed and simplified [to have a] greater focus on essential practical teaching skills* (LSIS, 2013, p 18) there are no suggestions that they will be removed.

Inherent in this first value is the notion of respect for learners and the expectation that you should respect each learner *individually and equally* (LLUK, 2007, p 2). Giving and receiving respect is wholly consistent with the principles of andragogy and learning in colleges. Some younger learners may have had negative experiences of life (and education) and may be unused to either giving or receiving respect. However, it is *essential that our own behaviour is a model that we would wish our learners to follow* (Wallace, 2007, p 56). This requires you as a tutor to be *enthusiastic, polite and committed* (ibid). Only if students are shown respect and this behaviour is modelled for them can they be expected to give respect to tutors.

The use of first names in colleges is one of the key ways in which FE distinguishes itself from schools and demonstrates colleges are *places where students [are] valued as equal partners in contrast to the strict hierarchical organisation of schools* (Peart, 2013, p 36). However, younger students need to understand that how they address you as a FE tutor may be different to how they address their school teacher and while they may seek to *test the boundaries* (Donovan, 2005, p 155), they need to appreciate that the way they speak to working adults may change according to venue and role. The use of first names may also create confusion for some students, who may believe this to be an invitation to become friends. While you may wish to be friendly towards students you are not the *learners' friend ... you're their teacher* (Wallace, 2007, p 97). Indeed there would be something deeply unsettling and potentially compromising about tutors working in a professional environment who chose to have their students as their friends. You need to be respectful of students' personal boundaries and not, in an effort to be friendly, pry into their personal lives. These boundaries need to be clear for both students and staff if appropriate professional relationships are to be established and maintained. The use of first names may be equally testing for some school teachers who could fear a breakdown of discipline and order and may have concerns about how students will manage this practice when they return to school.

CASE STUDY

Below is an extract from a letter produced by a school and distributed to pupils selected to take part in the IFP. Read the extract and then tackle the critical thinking task.

You have been selected to take part in an exciting initiative with Futures First College. You will be able to study a range of options while at the college which will enable you to gain valuable additional qualifications and will support you in pursing your chosen career. You will need to attend an induction event at the college on Wednesday 4th September at 2.00pm. You will return to school at 4.30pm. While you are not required to wear school uniform, appropriate dress must be worn. Offensive slogans or logos on clothing are not acceptable.

For this first visit, you will be driven to the college in the school minibus by Mr Smith. Mr Smith will remain with your group for the duration of the visit. I would like to remind you that while at the college you are a representative of the school and you are expected to adopt the highest standards of behaviour. Any pupil failing to meet these expectations will be reported to me and may not be allowed to return to college.

Congratulations on your selection and I hope you have a productive, informative and successful visit.

Critical thinking activity

»   *Who should take responsibility for organising an IFP induction visit?*

»   *What roles and responsibilities need to be agreed between the school and college prior to the visit?*

»   *What message should the school and college be seeking to give for a first visit?*

»   *What support should be offered to school students on their induction visit?*

»   *Can you identify any potential points of conflict between the school and the college regarding a letter like this?*

Adopting appropriate and consistent tutor behaviour

Successful professional relationships with students and staff, like any other relationship, require maintenance. A key feature of this maintenance is ensuring that you as a tutor act in an appropriate manner. It is important to remember that you are an adult and while learners may awaken feelings of anger where you feel roused to 'give as good and you get' or 'fight fire with fire', your adult and professional responsibilities prohibit you from behaving in this way.

A further key feature of maintaining positive relationships is consistency. Your students have the right to expect that when you are working, you will fairly apply college standards at all times. Your behaviour should not be predicated on your mood or other personal matters. As their teacher you should not have favourites who you excuse from meeting required learning standards like arriving to sessions on time. Nor should you apply standards in an apparently random fashion. If you have agreed with learners 10 minutes after the start of a lesson no students are allowed to join the group, you must apply this to all students. This applies to both the 15 year old who missed the bus and the 30 year old who had childcare problems that morning.

Both tutors and younger learners need complete clarity regarding professional boundaries and what are acceptable working practices. Sometimes, these boundaries can be blurred and tutors and students may, on occasion, cross these boundaries and put themselves in potentially difficult situations. A particular area of concern here is the expansion of technology in education and social networking sites. Students may send invites to tutors to be their 'friends' on social network sites. While this is not illegal or may not be against any professional guidance given by colleges, it is ill-advised to join the accounts of students. It could present a conflict of interests or, at worst, the tutor may find themselves accused of harassment or other unacceptable behaviour. To minimise this difficulty some colleges have set up monitored closed college sites which are a legitimate way for students to contact tutors or for tutors to contact students. Similarly, tutors may find that they have inadvertently joined to a student's account by tagging an image or other posting. This situation is further complicated by the fact that not all social network users use their own identity and may have established an alter-ego. Although it could be seen to limit net access for staff, some tutors have managed this concern by only having a professional net presence and only using dedicated sites for working professionals.

Field trips and offsite visits are particularly good opportunities to build or cement working relationships with young people. While these are excellent occasions to work in different ways with young people, it is important that ground rules and codes of behaviour are clearly set out for staff and students. This may be problematic when accompanying mixed age groups of 14-adult students. Those over 18 are legally allowed to purchase alcoholic drinks and may wish to do so. However, neither they nor you can purchase alcoholic drinks for students under the age of 18.

Critical thinking activity

While talking with a group of students in college, they inform you of some recent postings on a social networking site of a number of Mr Smith memes. In one of these memes, Mr Smith is pictured with his head on the body of a hippo, with the caption 'nice diet ... not'. Other postings are more graphic and more offensive. The students claim they do not know who is responsible for these postings.

» *What issues does this raise for the college?*

» *What action should the college take?*

» *What response should the college make to Mr Smith? How can the college protect its staff from such actions?*

» *What action should the college take towards the meme creator?*

Mixing with adults – loco parentis and duty of care

Colleges are responsible for the safety of all college users and are under a duty of care to ensure the security and to promote the well-being of staff, students and visitors. The duty of care standard differs from the *loco parentis* standard applicable to schools, under which schools are fully responsible for the safety and well-being of its students, in that college users are required that they adopt reasonable precautions to ensure their own safety. Onus is therefore shared between the college and the user. Significantly, if a young person studies in college for part of or their entire timetable, they are still the responsibility of the school as long as they remain on the school role, and *loco parentis* is not automatically transferred to the college.

When young people are in college:

> *If there are under-18 year-old pupils in a group with those over 18, the sessions must be under the supervision of an approved adult, in other words one who has a current valid police check, and this person is responsible for ensuring that other adults do not have substantial unsupervised access to the child.*
>
> (Donovan, 2005, p 159)

Normally while in college, the college tutor would assume the role of the supervising adult for the group, although commonly if the school teacher was present this role would be shared.

Critical thinking activity

> *While shopping during your lunch break in a local store close to the college where you work, a 15 year-old student you teach on the IFP in your college calls you over. You do not wish to appear rude, so you go over to talk with her. She is with her 17 year-old boyfriend who also attends the college. At the end of your brief conversation, her boyfriend states that he will be driving his girlfriend back to the college and offers you a lift.*

» *What issues does this raise for you?*

» *What are your responsibilities in this situation?*

» *What actions should you take?*

» *Are there any parties that need to be informed of this situation?*

» *Are there any potential conflicts of interest in this situation?*

» *Are there any potential issues of illegality?*

Discussion: safety issues

Professional boundaries exist for everyone's safety and security. It is vital they are maintained. Failure to do so could compromise your personal and professional integrity and put you and your students at risk. The growth of new technologies has produced new challenges for college staff to manage. Many tutors are now unwilling actors on YouTube, filmed on mobiles by their students and then posted on the net. Although some posts could be seen as youthful, harmless fun, the posting of the hippo-meme described earlier is more serious as it is intended to ridicule and humiliate. As adults, tutors may be expected to have the necessary resilience to cope with a degree of lampooning but they are also entitled to institutional support when boundaries are transgressed. In this situation, the college should try and find the perpetrator and, within the standard college procedures, allocate a suitable penalty which should be coupled with a clear statement to all college users warning them of the unacceptable nature of such behaviour. Even if detection of the individual(s) is impossible, at the very least a central college statement should be issued. The college could also usefully make specific reference to cyber-bullying in any student code of conduct.

With regards to accepting lifts from students, there is no illegality in the situation described. However, it would be ill advised to accept a lift as it may give the impression that you are more of a friend than a tutor. You also cannot know whether the car is properly insured and, should there be an incident, you would have some difficult explaining to do as a passenger. While reporting being offered a lift possibly is not required, it would be advisable to inform your line manager of this situation and that you refused the offer. If the student were then to report the circumstances inaccurately, you would have already taken appropriate action.

Learner entitlements and responsibilities

Students studying in college often have a clear view of their entitlements and have formed views on how colleges should meet their expectations. Equally, most colleges also have views on students' responsibilities. As a college tutor you need to guarantee stated entitlements and help students understand their responsibilities. To assist students and staff, many colleges have produced charters which identify entitlements and confirm student responsibilities.

Charters usually begin with a college mission statement which describes the principal aim of the college and then indicates the minimum service standards they will provide, followed by college expectations. The table below indicates some of the typical entitlements and obligations identified in many student charters.

Typical college charter	
Entitlements – the college will provide:	**Responsibilities – students are expected to:**
A safe, secure college environment that meets the learning needs of all members of the college community.	Respect the college facilities and to maintain the quality of the college environment.
Appropriate social, recreational and communal spaces for student leisure use.	Use college premises appropriately and appreciate the needs of other college users.
High-quality learning resources that meet the needs of learners and promote achievement.	Attend all taught sessions punctually, participate in learning opportunities and make good use of learning resources.
Specialised learner support to help students achieve their full potential.	Co-operate with any assessments and make full use of the support provided.
Inspiring teaching that supports students to succeed.	Attend sessions with the correct equipment and have a pro-learning attitude.

Typical college charter	
Entitlements – the college will provide:	**Responsibilities – students are expected to:**
A welcoming environment that recognises diversity and values each student as a unique individual.	Actively uphold the principles of equality and diversity and not to engage in anti-social or discriminatory behaviour.
A robust, accessible complaints procedure which enables college users to easily inform college management of areas of concern or problems.	Report any incidences of anti-social or discriminatory behaviour or misuse of college premises or equipment

Critical thinking activity

»   *What is your view on college charters?*

»   *What sort of college guarantees and student obligations would you like to see included?*

»   *Does your college currently have a college charter?*

»   *How was this developed?*

»   *Which stakeholders were included in the development eg schools?*

»   *What issues do charters raise in terms of social responsibilities and the emergence of surveillance cultures?*

»   *How do sanctions interface with rights and responsibilities?*

Qualifications available to younger learners in college

Simply because of their age, it is unlikely that students aged 14–16 will be studying advanced-level courses. These students are more likely to be studying entry-level courses, or courses at levels 1 and 2.

The Qualification and Credit Framework (QCF), which includes both Vocational Qualifications (VQ) and all other awards, was revised in 2009 to clearly *show employers, teachers and learners what someone (had) learnt and (could) do as a result of that achievement* (Ofqual, 2009, p 2). The new framework was designed to remove the confusion that had appeared as a result of the proliferation of qualifications offered in schools, colleges and work-based learning (WBL) environments. Level 3 qualifications, likely to be studied by those over 16, have also been included as a reference point. The general situation for 14–16 year olds studying in college is that they will follow NVQ-type qualifications or VQs from the QCF.

Qualification levels with examples

Level	Other qualifications Examples	QCF qualifications Examples
Entry	• Entry level certificates • Skills for life at entry level	Entry level VQs • Entry level awards, certificates and diplomas • Foundation learning tier pathways • Functional skills at entry level
1	• GCSEs graded D-G • NVQs at level 1 • Key skills level 1 • Skills for life • Foundation diploma	Level 1 VQs • BTEC awards, certificates and diplomas at level 1 • Functional skills at level 1 • OCR nationals • Foundation learning tier pathways
2	• GCSEs graded A*-C • NVQs at level 2 • Level 2 VQs • Key skills level 2 • Skills for life • Higher diploma	Level 2 VQs • BTEC awards, certificates and diplomas at level 2 • Functional skills at level 2
3	• AS/A levels • Advanced extension awards • International baccalaureate • Key skills level 3 • Cambridge international awards • Advanced and progression diploma	• BTEC awards, certificates and diplomas at level 3 • BTEC nationals • OCR nationals

(From Explaining Qualifications, 2009, p 7)

It is worth remembering that younger learners choosing (or being directed) to study NVQs and VQs at colleges may unwittingly limit their later life choices. While it is possible to move between academic and vocational routes and study level 4 or university-level qualifications in vocational subjects such as hairdressing and construction, there is an enduring, unresolved debate between the value and status of traditional academic and vocational qualifications. This debate is rooted in the 1944 Education Act, the same act which established the FE sector and produced a divided secondary school system of grammar schools for the academically able who followed a liberal, classical curriculum and modern schools which provided a more practical curriculum for other less academically able students.

Modes of study available to younger learners in college

Most younger learners who study in college will attend on a part-time placement through an agreed arrangement with their school. This might be attending for a single standard-length college session on a weekly basis as IFP students would or, exceptionally, on a full-time basis for those younger learners for whom school is totally unsuitable. Because of their age, transport and other constraints, regular college attendance is most likely to be during the daytime, consistent with standard patterns of school attendance.

Even if younger students do not attend college regularly, tutors may still be requested to work with these students through the following types of arrangement.

Types of working arrangements in use between FE colleges and schools

Type of contact	Appropriate uses
One-off visit	This may be used for some type of initial introductory contact. It may form part of a school's careers programme or may be part of a college's marketing strategy. This sort of contact could also be used by college or school staff who wish to gain greater awareness of the operation of either institution, or to complete fact-finding investigations.
Small-scale project	This may be used to develop some particular aspect of the curriculum, for example to provide sports students a chance to develop their football coaching skills with secondary school students, over a fixed time span. Organisations may choose this sort of working arrangement if resources or staff availability prohibits more sustained contact.
Occasional intermittent contact	This type of contact involves irregular contact between the two organisations. Cycles of contact could be termly or for longer time periods. This type of contact may be used for longitudinal project work, or could be part of a carousel of activities where school students gain experience in different college departments.

(Adapted from Peart and Atkins, 2011, p 76)

Some colleges have chosen to extend the opportunity for younger learners to attend without the formalised agreement of schools and have introduced 'junior academies'. To attend a college junior academy students apply direct to the college for a course without consent from their schools. These academies operate in a number of large conurbations including, for example, Birmingham, Ipswich, Reading and Nottingham, offering a range of courses such as catering, sport, dj skills and fashion. There is usually a fee for these courses payable by individual students, in contrast to college/school agreements when school students attend without incurring personal cost. Junior academy classes run outside of the standard school day and may take place in the evenings or on weekends. On successful completion of an academy course, colleges often award college certificates to recognise students' achievements.

The impact of youth on learning

Within our society many *conceptions of youth appear to be negative and critical, with young people viewed ... mainly as a source of trouble* (Marsland, 1987, p 5). Similarly, some government advisers also appear to hold negative views of young people and *the government's adviser on behaviour, former head teacher Charlie Taylor, told a committee of MPs that some pupils in England were too disruptive to fit into regular school life* (Sellgren, BBC News, 2013, online).

Young people experience a host of emotional, physical, psychological and cognitive changes as they *navigate the tortured period of adolescence* (Krotoski, The Observer, 2011, online); a time when they are obliged to *learn adult roles and acquire adult status* (Smith, 1987, p 41) and find a new, adult community where they belong. The combination of these changes can influence *self-concept and self-esteem, factors which themselves play a major part in motivation and learning* (Coleman, 1987, p 27). Sometimes, when young people

> *cannot find a place in their group through positive, cooperative behaviours they will often seek to achieve their aim by pursuing 'mistaken goals' [of]: 1. attracting attention; 2. demonstrating power; 3. seeking revenge; [and] 4. escape by withdrawal.*
>
> (Lee, 2011, p 74)

When young people choose to follow these mistaken goals in either college or school, they put themselves in direct conflict with the organisation and the authority figures within those organisations. This situation can be further complicated if college tutors and school teachers do not accept that young people are capable of expressing *sensitive and delicately balanced opinions* (Harkin, Turner and Dawn, 2005, p 140) and do not give young people an opportunity to express themselves constructively.

The challenge for tutors is to find ways to positively interact with young people and, rather than heading towards a mutually damaging collision, to recognise the impact of the maelstrom of adolescence and *find a solution that is acceptable to both parties* (Lee, 2011, p 70) and a way of working together towards reciprocally agreed goals. Only in this way can progress be made and *good working relationships* (ibid) maintained.

Critical thinking activity

Below is an extract of written feedback you have been given following a recent lesson observation of one of your literacy sessions with a class of 23 students who are studying an introduction to catering qualification. All students were between 16 to 22 years of age.

Overall this was an acceptable session, but there are a number of key points you need to pay greater attention to. Most students were actively engaged for most of the time. However, I was concerned your class seemed to have divided itself into several distinct enclaves. One of these enclaves consisted of the four youngest students in the class who seemed very reluctant to voice their views, with the exception of one 16 year old who repeatedly shouted out uninvited and unwanted comments. You appeared to try and tactically ignore these outbursts, but they were starting to visibly annoy the other students in the class.

» *What strategies would you adopt in this situation?*

» *How would you promote greater group integration?*

» *What rewards or sanctions would you consider using?*

» *What support would you want from your observer/college to help you address student behaviour in this class?*

Discussion: charters

In many ways, student charters are a development of existing policies and practices. They provide a formalised framework which explicitly articulates what colleges will provide and what students are expected to do when attending college. Student charters support codes of conduct and disciplinary procedures and by openly stating ground rules of expected behaviour, should support tutors. Ideally, charters should represent the views and interests of all stakeholders and during development colleges should seek to capture the views and feelings of students, staff, schools, business and other stakeholders. In this way the charter can be seen to be the property of all college users, rather than appearing to be a control mechanism introduced by the college management team.

Student integration

The academic and social integration of learners is a perennial challenge for all tutors. Often students will choose to sit in their preferred friendship groups and will be reluctant to integrate with other class users. In some regards it is wholly understandable that younger students may be hesitant to work with older class members. Older students may seem like authority figures and they could be concerned that there would be little shared, common ground. You will not be able to affect social groupings, but you can affect academic organisation. You could set up team tasks which required fully integrated groups, in which older and younger team members were required to work co-operatively to achieve academic goals. It would be a risky strategy to set up teams on a youth versus age basis as this could reinforce existing preconceptions or prejudices.

If a student is demonstrating socially unacceptable behaviour like constantly shouting out, you have a professional responsibility to tackle this behaviour. How you manage the situation needs to be based on your college code of conduct and your personal knowledge of the class. If at all possible, it would helpful if you could deal with this situation through humour. You might like to point out that although you are older, you can still hear perfectly well and there is no need to shout. However, while humour can be a useful way of diffusing a situation, you need to have a good understanding of your group because, used inappropriately, humour can be very damaging.

Being observed by a skilled observer can be very helpful. However, there needs to be clarity on the observation process. Is it part of a supportive peer feedback system in which colleagues can work together and share good practice, or is it part of a monitoring and checking procedure? While this may not affect what is seen in a lesson, it may affect how you respond to any feedback given. Assuming observations are part of ongoing staff development, you may like to ask your observer what strategies they have used to manage similar situations, or whether they can suggest other colleagues you could observe, so you can see how other tutors manage the situation; or whether they could lend you some training materials that would help you to improve your skill set.

Chapter reflections

Colleges have an evolving population of students and as a result of recent government changes are now catering for many more younger learners. Adolescence is a turbulent period and this change in student profile raises challenges for colleges, schools, tutors and students. It obliges all stakeholders to work together to negotiate an outcome where the needs of all parties are met. This requires creating co-operative solutions to practical issues such as timetabling, qualifications offered, modes of study and agreed approaches to discipline. To manage these difficult and competing agendas, colleges are making greater use of college charters and other frameworks which learners can buy into, which recognise the young person's status as a developing adult with choices and responsibilities.

LEARNING REVIEW AUDIT

Topic	I feel confident in doing this	This is an area I will need to develop
I can describe the historical background for young people studying in college		
I am aware of the challenges that young people face moving from mainstream schools to college		

Topic	I feel confident in doing this	This is an area I will need to develop
I can identify a range of useful strategies to support young people as they move from school to college		
I can list the different qualifications young people can study in college		
I can describe the different attendance patterns available to young people studying in college		
I understand some of the influences of adolescence on learning		

Taking it further

Hodgson, A and Spours, K (2008) *Education and Training 14–19, Curriculum, Qualifications and Organisation*. London: Sage.

Petty, G (2004) *Teaching Today*. Cheltenham: Nelson Thornes.

Pring, R et al. (2009) *Education for All – The Future of Education and Training for 14–19 Year Olds*. Abingdon: Routledge.

Race, P and Pickford, R (2008) *Making Teaching Work – Teaching Smarter in Post-Compulsory Education*. London: Sage.

Wallace, S (2008) *Teaching, Tutoring and Training in the Lifelong Learning Sector*. Exeter: Learning Matters.

Wolf, A (2010) Shifting Power to the Learner. *Adults Learning*, April 2010: 20–22.

www.teachingideas.co.uk/more/management/contents.htm

www.diploma-support.org/

www.ofqual.gov.uk

http://teachingandlearning.qia.org.uk/tlp/pedagogy/introduingthe1/index.html

References

Coleman, J (1987) Adolescence and Schooling, in Marsland, D (ed) *Education and Youth*. London: Falmer Press.

Department for Education (DfE), (nd), *Raising the Participation Age (RPA)*, HMSO. Available at www.education.gov.uk/childrenandyoungpeople/youngpeople/participation/rpa Accessed April 2013.

Donovan, G (2005) *Teaching 14–19: Everything You Need to Know About Teaching and Learning Across the Phases*. London: David Fulton Publishers.

Golden, S, O'Donnell, L, Benton, T and Rudd, P (2005) *Evaluation of Increased Flexibility for 14–16 Year Olds Programme: Outcomes for the first Cohort*. Nottingham: DfES.

Harkin, J, Turner, G, and Dawn T, (2005) *Teaching Young Adults: A Handbook for Teachers in Post-Compulsory Education*. Abingdon: Routledge Falmer.

Haydn, T (2012) *Managing Pupil Behaviour*. Abingdon: Routledge Falmer.

Hyland, T and Merril, B (2003) *The Changing Face of Further Education*. London: Routledge Falmer.

Lee, C, (2011) *The Complete Guide to Behaviour for Teaching Assistants and Support Staff*. London: Sage.

LLUK (2007) *New Overarching Professional Standards for Teachers, Tutors and Trainers in the Lifelong Learning Sector*. London: LLUK.

LSIS (2013) *Further Education and Skills in England: New Qualifications for Teachers and Trainers, Phase Two- Findings Report*. Coventry: Learning and Skills Improvement Service.

Lucas, N (2004) *Teaching in Further Education*. London: Institute of Education.

Marsland, D (1987) *Education and Youth*. London: Falmer Press.

Observer Newspaper (2011) Youth Culture: Teenage Kicks in the Digital Age. *Observer Newspaper*, 26 June 2011. Available at www.guardian.co.uk/technology/series/untangling-the-web-with-aleks-krotoski Accessed 24 April 2013.

Ofsted (2005) *Increased Flexibility at Key Stage 4*. London: Ofsted.

Ofqual (2009) *Explaining Qualifications,* Ofqual. Available at http://ofqual.gov.uk/qualifications-and-assessments/qualification-frameworks/levels-of-qualifications/ Accessed 8 May 2014.

Peart, S (2013) *Making Education Work – How Black Boys and Men Navigate the Further Education Sector*. London: Institute of Education Press.

Peart, S and Atkins, L (2011) *Teaching 14–19 Learners in the Lifelong Learning Sector*. Exeter: Learning Matters.

Sellgren, K. (2013) *Disruptive Behaviour Rising, Teachers Say*. BBC News, 23 March 2013. Available at www.bbc.co.uk/news/education-21895705?print=true Accessed 27 April 2013.

Smith, D.M. (1987) Peers, Subcultures and Schools, in D Marsland, (ed) *Education and Youth*. London: Falmer Press.

Vella, J (1994) *Learning to Listen, Learning to Teach*. San Francisco: Jossey Bass.

Wallace, S (2007) *Getting the Buggers Motivated in FE*. London: Continuum.

6 Meeting the needs of transient populations

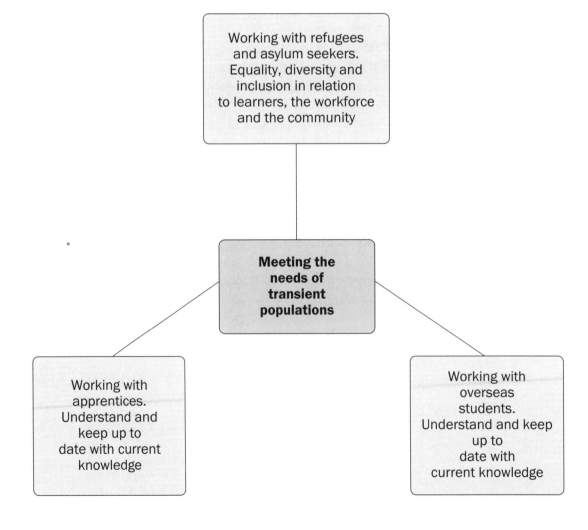

Chapter aims

Many colleges have fluctuating populations. These may include recent arrivals such as refugees, overseas students or learners studying apprentice programmes on block-release schemes. This chapter considers how colleges can meet both the academic and personal needs of this group which could include housing needs, pastoral care or medical support. At the end of this chapter, after you have worked through the different tasks and case studies you will be able to:

* specify some of the transient populations you may encounter;

* identify the sort of needs such populations may present;

* state what sort of support mechanisms these groups may need.

Working with apprentices

Why should we categorise apprentices as a 'transient population'? The answer lies in their required pattern of attendance. Those studying on day release may enjoy regular contact with the college; but those on block release will attend for a relatively short intense period of study and then it may be several months before they return for a further block. As a result, many apprentices have an intermittent and nomadic relationship with college and therefore need tutor support to help them to manage these transitions. Apprenticeships have long featured in the UK education system. Indeed, apprenticeship *has a history stretching back at least to medieval times* (Aldrich, 1999, p 14) and *after a period of decline in the 1970s ... this form of learning is enjoying a renaissance both in Britain and elsewhere* (Ainley and Rainbird, 1999, p 1). Historically, apprenticeships have *included both manual and professional pursuits ... although the main emphasis ... has been upon the former* (Aldrich, 1999, p 15), including traditional crafts such as joinery, engineering and masonry. Changes in employment patterns have increased the range of opportunities available to young people, and today it is possible to study apprenticeships in diverse occupations such as fitness instruction, financial services and ICT. With increased university fees, many young people are making a conscious and informed choice to follow an apprenticeship route, rather than incur considerable debt which they will have to repay later.

Apprentices form a unique cohort, being both company employees and company-sponsored college students. In the past, colleges have expected apprentices to *simply fit in with what was on offer* (Huddleston, 1999, p 185) and little attention was paid to the specific needs of either the company or the individual trainee. Today, best practice models mean that employers now work with colleges to design bespoke training packages which meet the company's *and* trainee's skills needs. Apprentices are based with their chosen company who pay them an agreed wage which must conform to national guidelines and attend the college for part of the time to access training. Employers and colleges work together to provide *relevant and realistic vocational education* (ibid) which clearly links theoretical learning to its practical application. Study patterns vary for apprenticeships and include both day-release and block-release models.

Apprenticeships provide an opportunity to develop skills in a specified field of employment and to earn a wage at the same time. Apprenticeships are open to anyone provided they are *16 or over, eligible to work in England [and] not in full-time education* (Gov.UK: online). During their nadir, apprenticeships were configured as *wasteful exercises in time-serving, oppressing youth labour* (Ainley and Rainbird, 1999, p 3) and only offering restricted low-level opportunities. However, contemporary apprenticeships are available at 3 levels from intermediate through to higher. The relationship of these levels to other qualifications is shown in the table below and indicates a similar progression time to standard academic qualifications. The length of apprenticeships varies depending on the level studied, but most apprenticeships take between 1 to 4 years to complete.

Apprenticeship level	Equivalent to	Likely time duration
Intermediate	5 GCSE passes	1–2 years
Advanced	2 A level passes	2 years
Higher	NVQ level 4; Foundation Degree Level	2 years

Adapted from Gov.UK: online

While studying for an apprenticeship, apprentices are able to gain valuable nationally recognised qualifications including NVQs at levels 2, 3, 4 or 5; numeracy and literacy qualifications; subject-specific technical certificates including BTEC and City and Guilds qualifications; and knowledge-based qualifications including Higher National Certificates (HNCs), Higher National Diplomas (HNDs) or Foundation Degrees (FdAs). Coupled with the opportunity to earn a wage as well as learning, apprenticeships have become a viable and attractive option for many young people.

Wages depend on age and employment status. There are currently four wage bands: Apprentice (this rate is for apprentices under 19 or those in the first year of their apprenticeship); Under 18s; 18 to 20 year olds; and 21 and over. It is important to note all apprentices are entitled to the national minimum training wage. In addition to a guaranteed minimum wage apprentices are also guaranteed 20 days paid holidays plus standard bank holidays.

Critical thinking activity

Brian is 17 and has been attending college for the past eight months as an automotive apprentice. He is based in a small garage that has a staff of six including the owner-manager, Paul, and Paul's partner, Claire, who takes care of the company's accounts and customer bookings. Paul takes great pride in 'looking after' his apprentices and Paul and Claire have been almost surrogate parents to previous apprentices. As the company is very small Paul can only afford to pay his apprentices the minimum training wage.

Brian recently came to see you and explained that although he was enjoying working for Paul and Claire, he had been offered a labouring job without training which would pay nearly double his current hourly rate. Brian told you he was unsure what to do and was torn between the loyalty he felt for Paul and the opportunity to earn more money. He asks for your advice.

» *What would you say to Brian?*

» *What factors does Brian need to include in his decision making?*

» *Log on to the government apprenticeships website to check the current rates of pay for apprentices.*

Discussion: career choices

Brian is currently facing a challenging career/employment decision. It is not your responsibility to make this decision for him, but it is your role to help Brian understand the full picture so he can make an informed choice. While the labouring job Brian has been offered pays considerably more money than his garage work, before making his choice Brian needs to know what job security the labouring post offers, how long the contract is for and the likelihood of the contract being renewed. Brian also needs to know if he will be employed as a full staff member or if he is being offered a less secure cash-in-hand post. It may be because the company is not paying tax or national insurance contributions for Brian that they can offer him a higher wage. It is also possible that the company may not have full employee indemnity insurance. This would be potentially very difficult for Brian if he were to be involved in an industrial accident and he may find that he is not entitled to compensation.

Brian also needs to know the potential impact of taking on an unskilled job. Apprenticeships offer the opportunity to gain valuable qualifications and gain relevant work-based experience. While he may benefit from short-term financial gains, he needs to be aware that successfully completing his apprenticeships would mean that over his working life he is likely to earn considerably more than other non-qualified workers. Once qualified, apprenticeships provide *a fantastic springboard for the future* (McLellan, 2013: online) enabling apprentices to gain either promoted positions with their current firms or to elect to move to other companies.

In reaching his decision Brian will need to consider these different factors and decide if he wants short-term financial gain or whether he will complete his automotive apprenticeship and have the opportunity of increasing his long-term employment opportunities.

Working with refugees and asylum seekers

On its website the United Nations High Commissioner for Refugees (UNHCR) defines a refugee as a person who:

owing to a well-founded fear of being persecuted for reasons of race, religion, nationality, membership of a particular social group, or political opinion, is outside of the country of his nationality, and is unable to or, owing to such fear, is unwilling to avail himself to the protection of that country.

(UNHCR, 1951, online)

In contrast, an asylum seeker is *someone who has applied for asylum and is waiting for a decision as to whether or not they are a refugee* (ibid).

Despite David Cameron expressing his uncertainty about the positive aspects of multicultural Britain in a speech he gave in 2011 (see chapter 7: *Race in education: the evolving multicultural debate*), the British Government states it has *a proud tradition of providing a place of safety for genuine refugees* (UK Border Agency, online). Further, the UK government states it will not return anyone to a *country where there is a real risk they will be exposed to torture or inhuman or degrading treatment or punishment* (ibid), thus positioning itself as a defender of the oppressed. Indeed some newspapers have made much of Britain's claim to be a safe haven and have suggested that Britain is overrun with refugees and bogus asylum seekers. However, figures from the UNHCR provide a very different picture in terms of the actual number of new asylum seekers entering the UK as shown in the table below. Consequently, although you may be responsible for teaching some asylum seekers, it is unlikely you will end up teaching large numbers of this group.

Global asylum applications

Country	Number of asylum applications for 2012
United States of America	70,400
Germany	64,500
South Africa	61,500
France	55,100
Sweden	43,900
United Kingdom	23,499 (figure for year ending June 2013)

Source: UNHCR, 2013, online

Many refugees and asylum seekers are keen to study at college and view education as a passport to a better life, holding *strong aspirations for the future, particularly in terms of … education and employment* (Refugee Support Network, 2012, p 6). Further, for those who have experienced traumatic life events *education provides a normalising routine which can help displaced people deal with the hardships endured both in their country of origin and en route to the UK* (ibid, p 7). The rules regarding *fee remission for refugees and asylum seekers are complex and subject to frequent change* (Doyle and O'Toole, 2013, p 5) resulting in some colleges giving confusing or contradictory advice or even refusing students' applications. For fees purposes, The Skills Funding Agency (SFA) states asylum seekers may be considered as home students, if they are *still waiting for a decision on their status after six months; they have been granted refugee status; have discretionary leave to remain; humanitarian protection; or have exceptional leave to remain.*

(Refugee Council Briefing, 2011, online)

Further they are entitled to full fee remission if they satisfy at least one of the following criteria:

- *In receipt of Jobseekers Allowance (JSA) or Employment and Support Allowance (ESA);*

- *Taking Adult Basic Skills or Functional Skills in literacy and numeracy other than English for Speakers of Other Languages (ESOL);*

- *Studying their first full level 2 qualification;*

- *Aged between 19–24 and taking their first full level 3 qualification.*

(ibid)

CASE STUDY

I started working at City College about five years ago as an ESOL tutor. Because of the location of the college, it always had an ESOL department and there was always an international group of students to teach. Mostly I taught older learners such as partners of Pakistani and Bangladeshi nationals and in more recent times European nationals from countries like Poland who had travelled here to work. Sometimes I had a refugee in my group, but this was only occasionally due to UK border entry criteria. For older learners, changes in fees and funding for ESOL courses often made it difficult for them to study. I enjoyed working with a multinational, culturally diverse group and found it very rewarding. Sometimes though, it could be very challenging and I remember one session with absolute clarity. Because of the international spread of English, many people arrive in the UK speaking some English and my role in college was to help them improve their English language skills. This was especially important if they wanted to apply for citizenship. It helped with mixing with other students at college and it clearly helped with living in the UK. Anyway I was teaching a level 2 ESOL course. Ashkir was in my group. Because he was 17, he received full fee remission. The course covered the usual things like speaking and listening, reading and writing and grammar. We had been doing work on homophones and I thought it would be a fun to play 'hangman' to guess the words. Ashkir, who was sitting near the front and was still waiting for his asylum claim to be processed, said 'that's how my uncle was murdered back home'. I don't play hangman with the students any more.

Critical thinking activity

» *How many students do you teach who could be described as refugees, asylum seekers or overseas learners?*

» *What training or support have you been given to help you meet the needs of these students?*

» *What do you consider are your personal training needs to enable you to work effectively with this group?*

» *What issues does the Ashkir case study raise for you?*

» *Have you experienced any critical incidents while working with refugees, asylum seekers or overseas learners?*

Working with overseas students

The United Kingdom is a popular study destination and attracts *over 430,000 international students ... every year* (University College and Admissions Service, UCAS: online) who study in both FE colleges and in HE. Overseas students may be divided into two basic groups. Those from the European Economic Area (EEA, formerly known as the European Union, EU); and international students, that is students from all other countries across the globe (excluding Bermuda and the Falkland islands which are classified as British Territories Overseas and whose population hold full British citizenship). There are important differences between these groups in terms of fee and visa status and potential cultural differences. The proximity of the EEA to the UK mainland, the increased movement of peoples, and for many EEA countries a shared alphabet, means many European citizens have some understanding of UK cultural practices. Although British Overseas Territories are geographically removed from the United Kingdom, these areas have an awareness of UK culture and practices which support transition to Britain.

If a UK education provider wants to teach international students, it must apply for a Tier 4 sponsor licence ... and must comply with a number of record keeping duties and reporting duties (United Kingdom Border Agency, UKBA: online). Duties include:

- *keeping a copy of the student's passport, biometric residence permit or UK immigration status document;*

- *reporting to the UKBA if the student misses more than ten sessions without prior permission;*

- *informing the border agency if there are significant changes in the organisation of your course, for example if the course is extended or shortened.*

(Adapted from UK Border Agency: online)

Many UK colleges now actively recruit both EEA and international students and have special arrangements to ensure a smooth transition to study in the United Kingdom. Students can study a wide range of courses including A levels, vocational courses, foundation and university courses. In addition to these full programmes, for students lacking the required language skills most colleges offer intensive English courses which are designed to ensure that students have reached the required literacy skills before beginning their programme. These language courses are often delivered during the summer break and depending on the skills level of the student last between 4 to 12 weeks.

In addition to the academic support needed by all students, most overseas students will require support with the following.

- *Accommodation:* Finding somewhere to live will be a priority need for many overseas students. While some students may be lucky enough to have family or other connections, often students choosing to study in the United Kingdom lack this level of support. As part of their student support services virtually all colleges now have dedicated accommodation officers who can recommend accredited rental properties and some colleges own a range of premises they can offer to students. College-recommended properties should meet minimum college standards which should include gas and electrical safety certification and basic minimum decoration standards. Some colleges may require additional assurances such as smoke or carbon monoxide detectors or accommodation entry phones. Colleges need to have clear criteria on who may apply for college-endorsed accommodation and should also have transparent rent-collection arrangements.

- *Health services:* While in the United Kingdom overseas students need to be able to access healthcare services. The United Kingdom Council for International Student Affairs (UKCISA) advises that *if your course of study is for six months or more … you will qualify for NHS treatment from the beginning of your course on the same basis as anyone who is ordinarily resident in the UK* (UKCISA: online). It is important to remember that not all countries adopt common immunisation procedures and overseas students may not have been vaccinated against measles, mumps and rubella (MMR) or hepatitis. You may wish to consider advising students to be vaccinated while they are in the United Kingdom. If students are studying for less than six months they will only be entitled to limited health care services and will need to pay for other services. For these students it is particularly important that they are informed that they must have appropriate private medical insurance which will meet the costs of any medical care they need.

- *Banking:* While studying in the United Kingdom students will need access to standard banking services. Many banks offer special student packages. If students have not set up a bank account prior to arriving in the United Kingdom they will need a letter of confirmation of course from their college to enable them to set up a bank account. This letter will need to state the student's full name, the course of study, the duration of the course, their UK address and their home address. The letter must be printed on college official stationary and signed by a staff member who has suitable authority; this would usually be the course tutor.

Overseas students may also require support with forming friendship groups while they are in the United Kingdom. Most colleges now have an international office, and as well as providing support with the above services, may have an international organisation that arranges social events to prevent students from feeling isolated. Some colleges may also have dedicated national groups such as the Caribbean Society or connections with the local University as a way of extending the support network available to students. You may also need to signpost students to particular spiritual support such as the local gurdwara or temple.

Discussion: safe havens

Every year college tutors meet new groups of students and every year college tutors are expected to meet the educational and pastoral needs of these students. In this respect, overseas learners, refugees or asylum seekers are no different from any other learners. They are simply new college students and they have the right to expect you will want to help them achieve their educational goals and aspirations. However, refugees, asylum seekers or overseas learners are not UK nationals and there will be differences between this group and the home students you teach. Nevertheless, your professional obligation to try and meet the needs of all the students you teach remains constant.

New entrants to the college and country can expect to be on a steep learning curve. They may need to acquire language skills, arrange for accommodation and understand a new currency. New entrants to the country will have to become familiar with a different set of cultural practices and behaviours. That which seems 'natural' and familiar to a UK national, may appear strange and incomprehensible to a foreign national. If you are to successfully support all your learners and if you are to provide a universally welcoming environment for all your students, you may need to revisit some of your personal practices and behaviours. Although games are an accepted teaching strategy that can help students to learn, when games become threatening or re-awake horrifying memories, they lose their educational value. A common word-game like hangman may have terrible connotations for some students and needs to be avoided. While it may be difficult to predict every trigger point for every student you teach, it is reasonable to expect you to review your teaching sessions to check if there are any potential areas of difficulty. If this is the case, your professional responsibility is to find an alternative teaching strategy for that particular topic. You could consider asking your students how they were taught a topic in their home country. This would be a way of demonstrating your positive acceptance of students and showing that you value the contribution they have to make to learning. Additionally it is a way of enhancing, enriching and refreshing the curriculum for the benefit of all learners.

Escaping

Considering Ashkir's needs, his throwaway comment immediately informs you of many important points. It appears that Ashkir has lived through, even if he did not directly witness, his uncle's hanging, a horrific, life-changing event. Has Ashkir been offered any counselling to help him with this issue? Does the college know if Ashkir and his family are being supported by the Refugee Council? Does Ashkir have a personal tutor and is his personal tutor aware of this event? While it is inappropriate to share all information with all staff, the fact that Ashkir has brought this issue up in class signals that he could accommodate some people knowing his situation and it is important that key people like his personal tutor are aware of his personal circumstances so that they may effectively support Ashkir while he is at college.

Not all colleges provide training for staff who work with international students and sometimes tutors need to find out information without college support. There are number of useful websites that tutors can access to help them. These include UKCISA, The Quality Assurance Agency (QAA) and UCAS. There may also be local support agencies you can access to help you.

Chapter reflections

Some student groups are easily overlooked as they may not be viewed as part of the mainstream college cohort. Overseas students, refugees, asylum seekers and apprentices are at risk as being seen as peripheral to the main student body. Indeed there are features of these student groups which almost work to make their integration more difficult and increase their invisibility. The very nature of these student cohorts means that they are often few in number, often form discrete social groups and may experience practical difficulties in integrating such as language barriers.

However, these groups are important to the wider agendas of all colleges. If colleges are to support government aims of providing safe haven to all genuine displaced peoples, they must ensure that they have systems in place to accommodate the needs of overseas students, refugees and asylum seekers. Colleges need to consider transition arrangements for these students and the links they have with other organisations such as the Refugee Council and the British Council which can support colleges in developing appropriate systems. These organisations can also help colleges to comply with existing legislation and advise them on document and audit trails they need to keep. Almost inevitably, much responsibility will be transferred to tutors in supporting these student groups; colleges need to assist teaching and other staff by providing regular, relevant training so that staff do not feel that they are left alone to manage situations. At the very least there should be a designated person or team with whom tutors can discuss any concerns they may have.

Apprentices are a key group in helping the United Kingdom to meet its current and future economic targets. They are significant in supporting industry and commerce to develop, form an important part of succession planning for the future, and are vital in filling industrial skills gaps. Many colleges are alert to the importance of apprentices and have worked with companies to help them develop relevant training packages. However, once again, college tutors are at the forefront of making these initiatives work and need college support to help them work with both employers and trainees. There are national organisations such as the Confederation for British Industry (CBI) who can work with colleges at a strategic level to help them develop their industrial links, and local organisations like East Midlands Development Agency (EMDA) that can support with practical implementation.

LEARNING REVIEW AUDIT

Topic	I feel confident in doing this	This is an area I will need to develop
I can name the different transient populations that attend my college		

Topic	I feel confident in doing this	This is an area I will need to develop
I can identify various needs of these student groups		
I can name internal college and external agencies that can support these differing student groups		
I know what my personal training needs are in relation to different student groups and where I can access information and training		

Taking it further

Allan, D (2013), *Refugees of the Revolution: Experiences of Palestinian Exile (Stanford Studies in Middle Eastern and I)*. California: Stanford University Press.

Barker, C (2011), *Choosing Your Apprenticeship*. Surrey: Trotman Publishing.

Dawson, C (2012), *Apprenticeships: For Students. Parents and Job Seekers*. London: Kogan Page.

Moorehead, C (2006), *Human Cargo: A Journey Among Refugees*. London: Vintage.

Philo, G, Briant, E and Donald, P (2013) *Bad News for Refugees*. London: Pluto Press.

Webber, F (2012), *Borderline Justice: The Fight for Refugee and Migrant Rights*. London: Pluto Press.

www.apprenticeships.org.uk Apprenticeships: Learning and Skills Council

www.cityandguilds.com City and Guilds

References

Aldrich, R (1999) The Apprentice in History, in Ainley, P and Rainbird, H (eds) *Apprenticeship: Towards a New Paradigm of Learning*. London: Kogan Page Limited.

Ainley, P and Rainbird, H (1999) *Apprenticeship: Towards a New Paradigm of Learning*. London: Kogan Page Limited.

Doyle, L and O'Toole, G (2013) *A Lot to Learn: Refugees, Asylum Seekers and Post-16 Learning*. London: British Refugee Council.

Great Britain *Apprenticeships from GOV.UK*. Available at www.gov.uk/apprenticeships-guide/applications-and-qualifications Accessed 15 December 2013.

Huddleston, P (1999) Modern Apprentices in College. So What's New? in Ainley, P and Rainbird, H (eds) *Apprenticeship: Towards a New Paradigm of Learning*. London: Kogan Page Limited.

McLellan, A (2013) *Learning as You're Earning: The Alternative to a Degree*. *The Independent*, Thursday, 30 May 2013. Available at www.independent.co.uk/student/career-planning/apprenticeships/ learning-as-youre-earning-the-alternative-to-a-degree-8637972.html Accessed 16 December 2013.

Refugee Council Briefing (2011) *Short Guide on Access to Further Education: Asylum Seekers and Refugees.* Available at www.refugeecouncil.org.uk/assets/0001/5918/FE_for_advisers_ guide_Aug_2011 Accessed 28 October 2013.

Refugee Support Network (2012) *I Just Want to Study: Access to Higher Education for Young Refugees and Asylum Seekers*. London: Refugee Support Network.

United Kingdom Border Agency (UKBA) *Asylum*. Available at www.gov.uk/browse/visas-immigration/ asylum Accessed 27 October 2013.

United Kingdom Border Agency (UKBA) *Adults Students – Tier 4 (General).* Available at www.gov.uk/ tier-4-general-visa Accessed 25 November 2013.

United Kingdom Council for International Student Affairs (UKCISA) *NHS Services.* Available at www. ukcisa.org.uk/international-Students/study-work--more/Health-and-healthcare/NHS- Services/ Accessed 26 November 2013.

United Nations High Commissioner for Refugees (UNHCR) (1951) *Convention and Protocol Relating to the Status of Refugees.* Available at www.unhcr.org.uk/?id=31 Accessed 27 October 2013.

United Nations High Commissioner for Refugees (UNHCR) (2013) *The Facts: Asylum in the UK*. Available at www.unhcr.org.uk/?id=31 Accessed 28 October 2013.

University College and Admissions Service (UCAS) *International.* Available at www.ucas.com/how-it- all-works/international Accessed 25 November 2013.

7 Working with cross-cultural groups

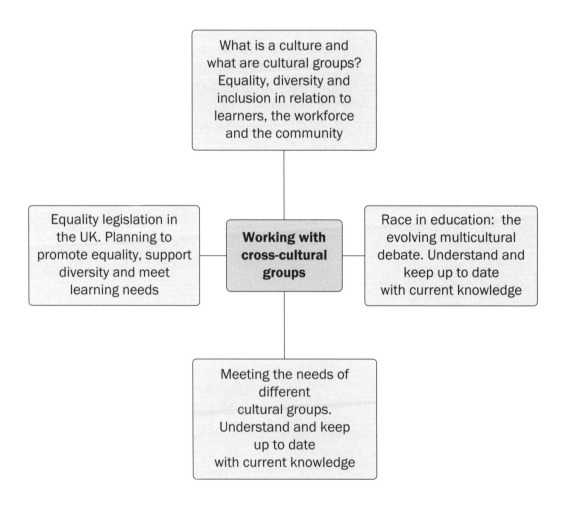

What is a culture and what are cultural groups? Equality, diversity and inclusion in relation to learners, the workforce and the community

Equality legislation in the UK. Planning to promote equality, support diversity and meet learning needs

Working with cross-cultural groups

Race in education: the evolving multicultural debate. Understand and keep up to date with current knowledge

Meeting the needs of different cultural groups. Understand and keep up to date with current knowledge

Chapter aims

This chapter examines the specific cultural needs of different college users. It provides a definition of culture and considers how tutors and colleges can choose to respond to these situations in order to meet the differing cultural needs of all college users. Questions raised through the case studies and critical thinking tasks are discussed in more depth later in the chapter.

Colleges bring together a range of different groups who will necessarily have a range of different needs and expectations. It is your job as a tutor, in collaboration with other college staff, to meet these diverse needs and to manage learners' expectations within the context of national legislation and local college policies. This chapter explores the implications of meeting these diverse needs for both tutors and students. By the end of this chapter you will be able to:

*   discuss with your peers and others what you understand constitutes a cultural group;

*   explain current UK equality legislation and explain its implications for your work in Further Education (FE);

*   engage with contemporary debates about multiculturalism;

*   identify how you will work with, and what actions you will take to promote the achievement of different cultural groups and build a cohesive college community.

What is culture and what are cultural groups?

Culture matters to us as it is one of the ways in which we come to know and learn about ourselves, about others and how others experience us. However, defining culture or identifying those that belong to a particular cultural group is a hard task for it includes features such as skin colour, race, ethnic origin, nationality, physical appearance, gender, age and sexuality; learned behaviours including customs and practices; mannerisms as well as belief systems like religion and political ideology; and social constructs. Culture has been and continues to be influenced by geographical and temporal boundaries, and in practice is commonly understood as the mores and accepted norms of a group of people. Culture provides an all-enveloping mantle which forms both the historic backdrop and the contemporary landscape of our being and represents the human embodiment and enactment of our hopes, aspirations and fears. It is the unspoken, unwritten code which pervades every aspect of our existence, being felt and understood by each one of its members. Culture can expose us to the richness of being human, but equally it can circumscribe our opportunities by imposing stereotypical expectations of individuals and groups.

Culture is more easily experienced than it is explained and is constantly changing, being responsive to and a product of externally imposed factors and internally generated features. Over time different cultures have interacted with other cultures and new forms of being and living have been produced. While some parts of our cultural identity may be more or less fixed, for example you may remain part of national culture throughout your life, you may be part of other cultures, for example youth culture, for only a defined part of your life. You may also make a conscious choice to move into or out of a certain cultural group. For example you may switch your political allegiances or you could choose to adopt a different faith position. Furthermore, cultures may fragment or fracture and although one centralised dominant culture may remain at the core of your lived experience, you could simultaneously belong to multiple sub-cultural groups. Two interesting examples here are Sir Chris Hoy the Olympic cyclist who describes himself as a British Scot identifying two nation states, and Dara O'Briain, the comic who confusingly describes his culture as Irish, Catholic Atheist, drawing on nationality, religion and philosophical ideology to define himself.

Britain has long been a culturally diverse community, bringing together different peoples from across the globe, sometimes in a planned, intentional way (for example government-supported mass migration from the Caribbean in the 1950s to help rebuild post-war Britain) and at other times in a more ad hoc fashion or as a result of accident or disaster (an example here includes the accommodation of approximately 27,000 Ugandan Asian refugees expelled by Idi Amin in the 1970s). In addition there have always been numbers of people who of their own volition have chosen to migrate to the United Kingdom. As a result of this constant and continuing movement of global populations, the people of Britain

> *can be traced back many centuries to the Angles, Celts, Danes, Huguenots, Jutes, Picts, Romans, Saxons and Vikings. Today's heterogeneity encompasses nationality, 'race' [and] ethnicity... The British have Irish, English, Welsh and Scottish nationalities as well as racial/ethnic origins that are African, Caribbean, Arab, Bangladeshi, Chinese, Guyanese, Indian, Latvian, Lithuanian, Pakistani, Polish etc.*
>
> (Anon, 2003, p 151)

Each of these distinct groups has their own distinct culture which has been preserved and transmitted by *interactive human community* (Thornton, 2006, online) and together, through mutual exchange new cultural norms have been created. The pace of cultural change has further been accelerated by recent technological advances which have facilitated communication between and across cultures.

Critical thinking activity

Read the short description below.

> *I am a daughter, granddaughter, sister, aunt, cousin, British, African and Caribbean, a member of the community ... Although I spend much of my time in the world of education, it is my heritage, not my professional title and position that is central to my identity. My family name tells me my place in Caribbean history. To be disconnected from that identity means losing out not only on the capacity to explain who I am to others but also the possibility of truly knowing myself.*
>
> (Sinclair, 2004, p 98)

» *Take a moment to think about your own cultural location and connections. How would you define and describe yourself?*

» *What, if anything, has changed with time? What, if any cultures, have you elected to join and which have you chosen to leave?*

> *Culturally where do you see yourself in the future?*

> *How do you believe your culture and cultural connections have influenced your work in college?*

CASE STUDY

Read the following account of the murder of Sophie Lancaster.

In the early hours of Saturday, 11th August 2009, Sophie Lancaster, 20, was walking home through Stubbylee Park in Bacup Lancashire with her boyfriend, Robert Maltby, 21. Sophie was on a gap year and had hoped to start an English degree at Accrington and Rosendale College. She was a bright student and had previously attended Bacup and Rawtenstall Grammar School. Both Sophie and Robert were part of the Goth subculture. As they walked through the park, Sophie and Robert were subjected to an unprovoked and sustained attack by a group of drunken teenagers. Robert was repeatedly kicked in the head until he fell unconscious. Sophie tried to protect Robert and pleaded with the teenage attackers to stop beating him. Her pleas were ignored and the gang turned on Sophie and subjected her to the same treatment, kicking her while she was on the ground and stamping on her head. The injured couple were assisted by other youths in the park who called for the emergency services and tried to tend to the couple's extensive wounds. When the emergency services arrived, Sophie's facial injuries were so horrific the paramedics had difficulty identifying she was female. The attack left both Sophie and Robert in a coma. While he eventually awoke from his coma, Sophie's injuries were so serious it was clear that she would never recover, and 13 days after the attack, her family agreed to switch off her life support.

Sentencing the teenage gang at Preston Crown Court, Judge Russell said the attack was 'an act of feral thuggery ... a hate crime against these completely harmless people targeted because their appearance was different' (BBC News, 2008, online). Two of the teenagers, Brendan Harris, 15, and Ryan Herbert, 16, were given life sentences for their part in the attack.

Critical thinking activity

> *What does this account tell you about culture in the United Kingdom today?*

> *Would you describe Goths as a culture or subculture?*

> *Do you feel that all cultural and sub-cultural groups should be protected by law?*

> *Whose responsibility is it to define and describe cultures or sub-cultures?*

Equality legislation in the United Kingdom

The Equality Act came into force in the United Kingdom on 1st October 2010 and was designed to:

• protect individuals and groups from unlawful discrimination at work, in education, when accessing goods and services and across society in general;

- simplify existing equality legislation and bring coherence to the different, separate equality acts. These acts included the 1975 Sex Discrimination Act, the 1976 Race Relations Act, and the 1995 Disability Discrimination Act and all later amendments to these Acts;

- strengthen existing equality legislation and extend the number of groups protected by law;

- make it much easier for individuals to complain about suspected unlawful discrimination.

The Act specifically identifies nine different characteristics which are protected by law, shown in the table below.

Protected characteristic	What this means
Age	Under the terms of the Act it is unlawful to discriminate against an individual because of their age. However, age can still be used as a discriminating factor when there is an existing legal justification. For example, on a film studies course, colleges could not simply ban 16 year olds on the basis that many of the films used had an 18-rating. Instead the college would have to identify other age-appropriate material to illustrate the topic. Similarly, colleges could not prohibit a pensioner from a zumba-fitness class on the basis they were too old, although they could, and should advocate caution if there was any potential health risk.
Disability	A person has a disability if they have a significant or long-term condition which creates difficulty for them in carrying out everyday activities. This condition may be either mental or physical. Under the terms of the Act, non-visible conditions such as diabetes, autistic spectrum conditions and mental health disorders are covered, as each of these may affect an individual's ability to carry out routine tasks. In a teaching context, this may mean certain activities like debates may not be suitable if an individual has mental health concerns as this could put the student under duress.
Gender reassignment	Gender reassignment describes the process of changing from one biological gender to another. Once an individual has declared they wish to change gender they are protected by the Act. Gender reassignment is a personal journey and may not necessarily include surgery to change a person's physical characteristics. Within an educational context once an individual has declared their intentions to transition from one gender to another they are entitled to access the amenities of their chosen gender. Within a college context this would mean being able to access chosen gender changing and lavatory facilities.
Marriage or civil partnership	Marriage is a legally binding union, originally between a male and a female, although the law has now changed to allow same sex marriage. Civil partnership is a legally recognised union for male/male or female/female couples. Under the law, civil partners must now be treated in the same way as married couples for a variety of legal issues. For example on college enrolment forms civil partners would have to be recognised as the next of kin. Marriage is a legally binding union between a male and a female and from 29 March 2014 same sex couples can also legally marry. Further legislation expected to be adopted in 2015 will allow same sex couples who earlier entered civil partnerships to convert their union to marriage if they wish to do so.

Protected characteristic	What this means
Pregnancy and maternity	Pregnancy refers to the biological condition of expecting a child. Maternity is the period immediately after giving birth and lasts for 26 weeks. Protection is also provided to women who miscarry or who have a still birth. During this time, women are protected against maternity discrimination. In colleges this could mean allowing a nursing mother out of class to express milk to relieve discomfort or if infants are allowed on college premises, providing suitable facilities for breast-feeding mothers. However, it is important to note that breast feeding cannot be prohibited in public places and a college could not ban a nursing mother from breast-feeding her child in the college refectory. Many colleges have separate policies regarding children on college premises and colleges may need to review these policies to ensure their policies are consistent with contemporary Equality legislation.
Race	Race is used to describe a group of people who form a distinct and recognisable group and who share certain features or characteristics as defined by their colour, ethnic origin, or nationality. Race may include one or more of these features, for example 'Black British'. Colleges may need to consider how they provide support for groups such as the Black, Asian and Minority Ethnic (BAME) students.
Religion or belief	Religion involves living according to a defined set of principles prescribed by a given doctrine and acknowledging an ultimate divine power. Belief can include religion but also includes a broader set of organising principles such as Atheism or other philosophical positions such as Humanism. Both religion and belief will have a significant impact on the way that an individual chooses to live in society. Colleges may make specific accommodations for religion such as only using halal meat in its kitchens.
Sex	This describes an individual's biological gender. Men and women's rights are protected by the Act. For example, a male and female head of department would both be entitled to the same pay.
Sexual orientation	The act protects heterosexuals, lesbian, gay and bi-sexual people. The Act does not protect deviant forms of sexuality such as paedophilia or necrophilia. In a college context this may mean being alert to and mindful of discrimination such as homophobic 'joke-telling' or pejorative sexual insults.

Critical thinking activity

» *Having read the table above which identifies the nine protected characteristics, what advantages other than the ones listed at the start of this section can you identify of a single Equalities Act?*

» *What are the potential tensions that exist within the Act? For example, how should colleges accommodate fundamentalist religious views which do not support the rights of women?*

» *How should colleges determine precedence of one characteristic over another? Is this a role for colleges or should such issues be dealt with elsewhere? If so, what would be the appropriate organisation(s) to manage these challenges?*

» *What college systems need to be in place to ensure there is parity of treatment for all nine protected characteristics?*

» *What institutional support do colleges need to guarantee that the legislation is applied fairly to all groups?*

» *What, if any, additional characteristics do you believe should have been included in the legislation?*

CASE STUDY

At the end of one of your lessons Jade, a 17 year-old White British student asks you to accompany her to the student female toilets to see some graffiti before it is removed. You ask her why she cannot take a picture of the graffiti and she informs you there is simply *too much stuff* and she wants you to see *it with your own eyes*. You are hesitant, but agree to her request. On the back of toilet doors and by the mirrors you observe a number of hand-written notes which state things like *jade screws rag-heads*, *towel-head lover jade* and *white-trash traitor*. Some of this graffiti is outside of your slang understanding and you have to ask Jade to explain what it means. Jade explains that she has recently started going out with a British Asian Sikh and *rag-heads* and *towel-head* are pejorative terms used to describe Asians, derived from the fact that some Asians wear turbans. She tells you that some of the other female students think that she should only have White, British boyfriends. She also tells you she has also had a number of text messages in a similar vein which she has deleted. Jade believes she has a good idea of who is responsible for the graffiti.

Critical thinking activity

» *What are the different cultural groups you can identify in this situation?*

» *Reflecting on the 2010 Equality Act, which protected characteristics do you believe have been contravened?*

» *What is your immediate reaction to this scenario and what are your feelings?*

» *Would you agree to accompany Jade to the female toilets, and if not, why?*

» *What would you say to Jade?*

» *What would you do in this situation?*

» *What issues does this scenario raise for Jade, the lecturer in college and the college itself?*

» *What does this situation tell you about cultural awareness within the college?*

» *What are the apparent training needs for the staff and students in this situation?*

» *Who, if anyone, should this event be reported to?*

» *What immediate action should the college take?*

» *What longer-term actions does the college need to take?*

Discussion: cultural location

Membership of a cultural group can, for its group members, be fatal. This has been clearly illustrated in the United Kingdom by the Race riots in the 1950s, 1980s and more recently the murder of Stephen Lawrence in 1993. Membership of, or association with, certain cultural groups can be dangerous and comes with significant personal risk. Jade, by choosing to go out with a Sikh, became a target. Although not physically attacked, she was the victim of aggression and you as a tutor employed by the college would be obliged to take some form of action. As a racist incident, at the very minimum, this event must be logged and recorded. On a personal basis, as Jade has chosen to show you the graffiti and tell you about the event, you would appear to be in a good position to offer Jade some moral support at this time. While it is right that the offensive graffiti must be removed, removal alone is not sufficient. Although not necessarily your job to find out who wrote the graffiti, the college should try to discover who was responsible and should certainly restate its institutional opposition to all forms of racism and its commitment to producing a safe, secure environment for all college users. This may also include development days for students and staff alike.

By contrast, Sophie Lancaster, whose murder, discussed earlier in this chapter, was described by the Crown Prosecution Service as *truly shocking* for its *utter pointlessness and sheer brutality* (BBC News, 2008, online), was not a member of a minority ethnic community or religious group; Sophie Lancaster was a White British citizen and would in most circumstances be more usually described as part of the mainstream culture. And yet, Sophie Lancaster was murdered for belonging to the 'wrong' cultural group, leading her mother and family members to campaign for Goths and similar sub-cultures to be afforded the same safeguards as other protected characteristics identified in the 2010 Equality Act. Although this was not adopted nationwide, in 2013 Greater Manchester Police stated they would record *offences against members of alternative subcultures in the same way they do attacks based on race, religion, disability, sexual orientation or transgender identity* (The Guardian, 2013, online). This is a small victory for Sophie's family and will not bring her back; but it is recognition that violence against cultural groups is abhorrent and raises a challenge for colleges and other institutions about how to provide a safe, secure environment for everyone.

Because cultures change and evolve, and new cultures may emerge, defining *all* cultures and cultural groups at any given point is and will remain an enormous challenge. Cultural location and/or affiliation can be dangerous and can produce the most serious crimes. Colleges have both a legislative responsibility and a moral obligation to uphold and enforce these policies so that students can learn and tutors may teach.

Race in education: the evolving multicultural debate

Internationally multiculturalism has a long history. The first countries which defined themselves as multicultural societies were those with *long, historical experience of immigration and indeed which have been built up out of immigration, namely, Canada, Australia and the United States* (Modood, 2013, p 3). Canada was the first government to *adopt multiculturalism as official policy in 1971* (Race, 2011, p 3) and their government still openly supports this policy. On the Canadian Government immigration website it declares

> *Multiculturalism ensures that all citizens can keep their identities, can take pride in their ancestry and have a sense of belonging. Acceptance gives Canadians a feeling of security and self-confidence, making them more open to, and accepting of, diverse cultures. The Canadian experience has shown that multiculturalism encourages racial and ethnic harmony and cross-cultural understanding, and discourages ghettoization, hatred, discrimination and violence.*
>
> (Government of Canada, online)

However, other Western economies have been less supportive of multiculturalism. In 2010 the German Chancellor, Angela Merkel, stated that multiculturalism and an attempt to *live side-by-side … had utterly failed* (BBC news, online). In an overt move to the right, Merkel also stated that educating unemployed Germans should take priority over recruiting foreign workers and that immigrants should *do more to integrate into German society* (Weaver, 2010, online). Similarly, the British Prime Minister, David Cameron, also indicated his concern over multicultural policies, claiming in a 2011 speech that:

> *Under the doctrine of state multiculturalism we have encouraged different cultures to live separate lives, apart from each other and apart from the mainstream … We've even tolerated these segregated communities behaving in ways that run completely counter to our values … We need a lot less of the passive tolerance of recent years.*
>
> (Cameron, 2011, online)

CASE STUDY

The extract on the following page describes a 50-minute observation of a BTEC sports science class. A diagram of the room organisation is provided for reference. Twelve students attended the session.

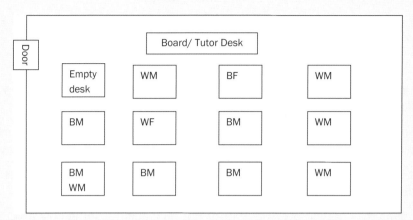

Key: WF = White Female; WM = White Male; BF = Black Female; BM = Black Male

Standard classroom session. Group assembled outside of class 15 minutes before scheduled session. Group engaged in conversation with personal tutor (a White male) who used time before taught session to catch up with his group and check general progress. Group fully attentive to their personal tutor during this time. Class tutor (also a White male) arrived 10 minutes late. Group entered class. Session taught by usual tutor. Tutor gave initial instructions for session. Chatting from 3 BMs during instructions. Tutor said 'boys, boys' and chatting stopped. Tutor asked group general questions. Answered by 4 BMs. Tutor satisfied. Group understood work and all students began working on the initial task. Some chose to complete task individually, others chose to work with friends. There was no mixing between genders and only mixing between Black and White students was 1 BM and 1 WM at back of class. All students worked on task as instructed. Tutor circulated around class. Tutor brought activity to close. Tutor asked questions of group. Questions answered in turn by BM, BF and BM. Tutor gave public praise to students. Tutor gave further input, using board to draw illustrations of relevant techniques. Group made notes. More tutor questions answered by BF, BM, BM and BF. Tutor then asked a very challenging question to class. Group silent for some time (approx 20 seconds) then 1 BM hesitantly answered. More public praise by tutor to those who answered questions. Tutor then gave information on what was needed to gain a distinction for assignment. Group took notes. Clarification questions asked by 3 BMs. Tutor moved onto next set of instructions which involved moving room to computer suite. Some restlessness and group seemed ready to move on. 1 WM asked clarification question. 1 BM asked further question. Tutor answered. 3 WMs noticeably restless by now. Tutor needed to settle group so he was assured students were ready to continue working in computer suite. Once satisfied, tutor allowed group to leave for computer suite.

Critical thinking activity

» *What are your observations about the cultural organisation of this class?*

» *How culturally cohesive does the group appear to be? Is there any suggestion of classroom ghettoisation?*

» What, if any, points would you be concerned about?

» What advice, if any, would you give to the group's personal tutor and their class tutor?

» How culturally cohesive are your classes?

» What do you do to promote positive relationships between groups and how do you simultaneously show respect for different cultural practices?

» On a personal basis, are there any cultural practices which, like David Cameron, you find difficult to accommodate? How does this view impact on the way that you teach?

» What training or staff development activities have you been able to access to help you develop your understanding of different cultural norms?

While politicians may debate over whether or not multiculturalism is desirable, it is a fact that Britain is home to a number of different cultural groups and that currently *the ethnic minority population is increasing* (National Audit Office, 2008, p 4). As a result of this, individually, institutionally, locally and nationally we will all need to determine how we are going to live and work in the diverse Britain of the twenty-first century. Education has been and continues to be a significant part of this debate and has the opportunity to engage with students and communities to help generate future solutions. In the secondary sector, citizenship has provided structured opportunities to teach *subjects [like] racism, terrorism and anti-discrimination* (Race, 2011, p 11). FE has no such prescribed curriculum and often it is the responsibility of individual tutors to work out how they will teach and work with culturally diverse student groups.

CASE STUDY

In 2013 as part of a move to improve security, Birmingham Metropolitan College stated that when on college premises students were forbidden to routinely cover their heads or faces by wearing hoodies, hats, caps or veils. This move was taken by the college management team so that students were clearly recognisable at all times. The college's actions were supported by the Prime Minister, David Cameron, who stated that each institution should be free to set its own dress code policy, but Nick Clegg, the Deputy Prime Minister did not support this view stating:

> as a general principle, other than … exceptional circumstances, [he was] really quite uneasy about anyone being told what they have to wear.
>
> (BBC News, 2013, online)

However, in September 2013 after further representations the college decided to reverse its decision to allow students to wear *specific items of personal clothing to reflect their cultural values* (ibid).

Critical thinking activity

»   *What position has your college adopted in relation to wearing religious dress or other symbols? Does this apply equally to all college users including children in the college creche, students, academic staff, support staff, contractors and visitors to the college?*

»   *What issues do the positions taken by David Cameron or Nick Clegg raise for colleges who are duty bound to implement the Equalities Act?*

»   *What support might colleges require to help them navigate the apparent contradictions between the public statements of politicians and their legislative duties?*

»   *What is your personal position in relation to openly indicating a personal religious belief while engaged in college business? What potential difficulties might declaring your belief position create for either you or your students? Are there any conflicts of interest and, if so, how might these be resolved or accommodated?*

Discussion: building college communities

Tutors are at the sharp end of legislation and policy implementation. They are obliged to identify the inherent contradictions in these frameworks and to resolve these difficulties, for the mutual satisfaction of all users and stakeholders. Politicians have the luxury of making grand statements; tutors and colleges have the challenge of making these statements work. Education has a key role to play here and either by syllabus based or incidental opportunities, colleges are charged with combating *stereotypical thinking relating to minority communities* (Race, 2011, p 48). While individuals may for cultural or other reasons (for example personal safety) prefer to associate with those who are like them, colleges and therefore by implication tutors, are given the bigger challenge of building a socially cohesive society. Most minority communities have vigorously resisted the *assimilationist social policies* (ibid, p 16) of the 1960s where minority communities were forced into adopting the social norms of the host majority and wish to retain their own distinct cultural identity. Consequently, minorities may elect to form discrete enclaves within wider mainstream culture and to preferentially associate with others whom they identify as 'one of them'. However, on occasions tutors need to disrupt this preferred default positions and ask students to work with others whom they would not normally work with. Through this disruption different groups by mutual exchange can learn more about each other and thereby are given the opportunity to develop greater understanding of different and diverse cultures. Contact reduces the boundaries of 'us' and 'them' and has a role in making the unfamiliar less strange and exotic.

At an institutional level, colleges need support in helping to build cohesive communities and need to establish local and national support to help them achieve this goal. This could include forming networks with organisations like the Citizens' Advice Bureau, The Department for Communities and Local Government, the Home Office and the Immigration and Border Agency.

Although only very small gestures, it is acts like these that help to dismantle the architecture of segregation and help to build socially cohesive communities.

Chapter reflections

Colleges are charged with respecting and protecting the rights of individual students and of different groups. This means that you need to understand what culture means and what constitutes a cultural group. This is not simple as the features of a cultural group are not necessarily fixed, and allegiance to certain cultural or sub-cultural groups may be, at least to a degree, a matter of choice. You need to understand what could be considered a permanent cultural group (for example, it is not possible to change your ethnic origin), and those groups which may be transient (for example, allegiance to a particular youth culture). You need to understand which groups receive statutory protection and which groups are not afforded such protection. Within a college context, it is very possible you, as a member of staff, will be obliged to resolve difficulties between different cultures or different factions. You will need to have a clear understanding of your own beliefs as this will impact on how you respond to a situation and what you choose to do. You will also need to understand how your college has interpreted legislation, what systems are in place to support different groups and what expectations the college has of you as a college employee.

LEARNING REVIEW AUDIT

Topic	I feel confident in doing this	This is an area I will need to develop
I have an understanding of the different features of culture and I can identify different cultural groups within college		
I am familiar with current equality legislation in the United Kingdom and appreciate some of the challenges in implementing this legislation		
I am aware of the UK position and some global responses regarding race and education		
I have a good understanding of my personal position with regards to race and education		
I have considered what helpful strategies I could use when working with mixed cultural groups to promote positive relationships between different groups		

Taking it further

Brighouse, H, Tooley, J, Howe, K.R., and Haydon G. (eds) (2010) *Educational Equality*, London: Contiuum.

Garratt, D and Forrester, G (2012) *Education Policy Unravelled*. London: Continuum.

Peart, S (2013) *Making Education Work: How Black Boys and Men Navigate Further Education*. London: Trentham Books and the Institute of Education Press.

Terzi, L (2010) *Justice and Equality in Education*, London: Continuum.

www.globaleducation.edu.au/ Global Education

www.gov.uk/equality-act-2010-guidance Government Equalities Office

www.unesco.org/ United Nations Education, Scientific, Cultural Organisation

References

Anon (2003) *Cultural Diversity Guide*. London: Granada PLC.

BBS News England (2008) *Boys Sentenced over Goth murder*. Available at http://news.bbc.co.uk/go/pr/fr/-/1/hi/england/lancashire/7370637.stm Accessed 19 October 2013.

BBC News, (2013) *Birmingham Metropolitan College Decides on U-turn Over Veil Ban*. Available at www.bbc.co.uk/news/uk-england-24072854 Accessed 12 October 2013.

BBC News (2010) *Merkel Says German Multicultural Society Has Failed*. Available at www.bbc.co.uk/news/world-europe-11559451?print=true Accessed 6 October 2013.

Cameron, D (2011) *PM's Speech at Munich Security Conference*. Available at http://webarchive.nationalarchives.gov.uk/20130109092243/http://number10.gov.uk/news/pms-speech-at-munich-security-conference/ Accessed 6 October 2013.

The Guardian (2013) *Manchester Police to Record Attacks on Goths, Emos and Punks as Hate Crimes*. Available at www.theguardian.com/uk/2013/apr/03/manchester-police-goths-pinks-hate-crime/print Accessed 20 October 2013.

Government of Canada (nd) *Canadian Multiculturalism*. Available at www.cic.gc.ca/english/multiculturalism/multi.asp Accessed 6 October 2013.

Modood, T (2013) *Multiculturalism*. Cambridge: Polity Press.

National Audit Office (2008) *NAO, Increasing Employment Rates for Ethnic Minorities* London: The Stationery Office (TSO).

Race, R (2011) *Multiculturalism and Education*. London: Continuum.

Sinclair, M (2004) Listening to Parents: Striving to Succeed – An Action Research Project on Highly Achieving African Caribbean Pupils, in *Equal Measures –Ethnic Minority and Bilingual Pupils in Secondary Schools*, Travers, P and Klein, G (eds) Stoke-on-Trent: Trentham.

Thornton, C and Jaeger, A (2006) Institutional Culture and Civic Responsibility: An Ethnographic Study. *Journal of College Student Development*, 47: 52–68.

Weaver, M (2010) *Angela Merkel; German Multiculturalism Has Utterly Failed*. Available at www.theguardian.com/world/2010/oct/17/angela-merkel-german-multiculturalism-failed/print Accessed 6 October 2013.

8 Integrating offenders in Further Education

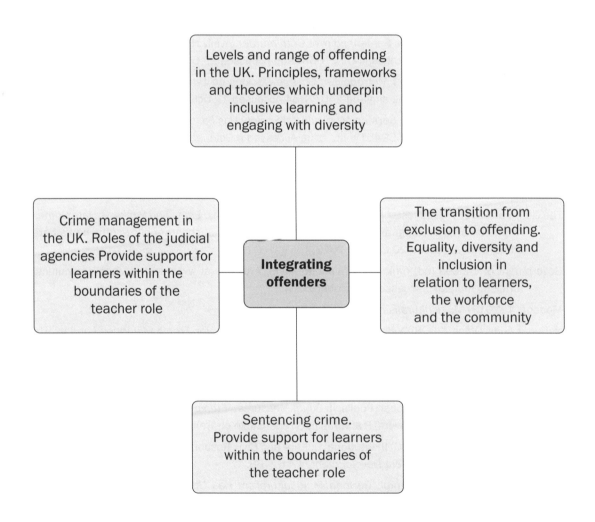

Levels and range of offending in the UK. Principles, frameworks and theories which underpin inclusive learning and engaging with diversity

Crime management in the UK. Roles of the judicial agencies Provide support for learners within the boundaries of the teacher role

Integrating offenders

The transition from exclusion to offending. Equality, diversity and inclusion in relation to learners, the workforce and the community

Sentencing crime. Provide support for learners within the boundaries of the teacher role

Chapter aims

From its very beginnings FE has aimed to support personal development for individuals and communities and *provide a second chance* (Foster, 2005, p 5) for learners who want or need to access education. As such, FE has ideologically positioned itself to support marginalised groups, including those who may have entered the criminal justice system at some stage. Because of the wide age range of students attending colleges (and indeed the range of FE provision inside secure institutions), as a tutor you could find yourself teaching both juvenile and adult offenders.

This chapter considers how offence and offender management has changed in the United Kingdom and the implications of this change for students and tutors. Many offenders are now managed within the community and, rather than being given a custodial sentence, serve all or part of their sentence in the community, possibly being managed by having an electronic tag fitted. Education may form an integral part of their rehabilitation and they could be expected to participate in different education programmes offered either by mainstream colleges or the National Probation Service (NPS). This change in offence management raises issues for offenders, tutors and other students. Such issues need to be managed proportionately and tactfully. These are challenging issues and all college users need to be clear on the roles, responsibilities and boundaries that exist when working with students who have an offending record.

After reading this chapter and completing the critical thinking tasks, you will be able to:

* describe the scope and levels of offending in the United Kingdom;

* explain the transition from exclusion to offending;

* identify the range of judicial agencies that students could have contact with;

* describe the range of different sentencing options.

Offending in the United Kingdom

Newspaper headlines such as *UK is Violent Crime Capital of Europe* (Edwards, Daily Telegraph, 2 July 2009) compared to *Crime at Its Lowest Level for 30 Years* (Travis, The Guardian, 25 April 2013) and *Britain's Crime Hotspots: Astonishing Figures Identify the Most Lawless Postcodes in the Country* (Beckford, Cooper and Hall, Daily Mail 10 August 2013) give a confusing and contradictory picture of the level of crime in the United Kingdom. Young people in particular are often portrayed as actively engaged in criminal behaviour with especially inflammatory headlines like *Violent Youth Crime Up a Third* (Leapman, The Daily Telegraph, 20 January 2008) and *Under 18s Commit a Quarter of All Crimes* (Doyle, The Daily Mail, 20 May 2012). Reports of this kind have helped to *elevate concern regarding the anti-social activities of young people into a chronic moral ferment* (Stephenson, 2007, p 52) and create the impression that many young people are out of control.

While such sensationalist reporting may help to sell newspapers, official Home Office fig-ures for 2012–13 show recorded crime in England and Wales (with the exception of sexual crimes) have fallen for all offences as indicated in the table below.

Offence type	Number of offences		Percentage change
	2011–12	2012–13	
Violence against the person	626,720	601,134	-4.1
Sexual offences	52,760	53,540	1.5
Robbery	74,688	65,158	-12.8
Theft offences	2,013,428	1,850,156	-8.1
Criminal damage and arson	626,008	529,719	-15.4
Drug offences	229,099	208,017	-9.2
Possession of weapons	23,688	19,913	-15.9
Public order	150,858	132,203	-12.4
Miscellaneous crimes	44,981	42,483	-5.6
Totals	3,842,230	3,502,320	-8.8

Home Office Statistical Bulletin, 2013, p 14

Although actual crime figures may have fallen, popular perceptions of lawlessness and crim-inality, fuelled by dramatic reporting, persist, creating a climate where

> *most members of the public feel that the level of crime is rising. Two out of three adults feel that crime has increased nationally while around one in three believes it has increased locally. Different age groups perceive this differently; young people are more likely to say that crime has increased locally, while older groups are more likely to believe crime has increased at a national level.*

> (Victim Support, 2011, p 7)

As a tutor, your responsibility is to manage the hyperbolic claims of the press, be aware of the reality and calm potential reactive responses from students and staff.

Background to offending

While there are no agreed definitive causes for offending, many educationalists and crimi-nologists recognise a number of factors which can increase the risk of an individual turn-ing to crime. The two basic theories regarding the causes of criminality relate to personal responsibility and societal structure.

Personal responsibility factors which may increase the likelihood of individuals adopting a criminal lifestyle include the following.

- *Lack of self control*: Some individuals appear to have great difficulty in managing themselves and understanding the potential consequences of their actions. They may display behaviours such as *impulsiveness [and] risk taking* (Stephenson 2007, p 6) and are easily persuaded to act with a group or to carry out actions to maintain their credibility with their peers.

- *Low academic ability:* The UK education system is structured on linear attainment targets which students are expected to achieve by certain ages. Those that do not achieve these targets may find education hostile, challenging or irrelevant and feel excluded from the system. Some may choose to disengage from education entirely and to pursue other targets where they can be successful. This may include participating in crime. While low academic ability does not necessarily cause offending, the Prison Reform Trust noted that *half of all prisoners were at or below Level 1 (the level expected of an 11 year old) in reading; two-thirds in numeracy; and four-fifths in writing* (2003, p 6), suggesting that those with lower academic ability are more at risk of engaging in crime.

- *Poor attendance*: Truancy does not cause criminality but represents a *significant risk factor in criminal careers* (Newburn and Shiner, 2005, p 26). The Prison Reform Trust also found *prisoners [were] ten times [more] likely to have been a regular truant* (2003, p 6) when in education. Truancy implies a lack of supervision and therefore provides the opportunity to offend.

Societal factors potentially contributing to criminality include the following:

- *Labelling theory*: Labelling theory describes a process where individuals or groups are labelled in some way. This may be as low-achieving, disruptive or criminal. Tutors may expect little of these groups and are not surprised when they learn they have been engaged in offending. Tutors' responses to these groups are influenced by their pre-existing low expectations, leading to offering less support, so lowering attainment further and thus re-enforcing tutor expectations and allowing the cycle to continue. Some students may feel they have 'nothing to lose' by engaging in criminal activity as they have already been identified as a problem and crime could be an area where they can experience success.

- *Lack of opportunity*: As an extension to labelling theory, when groups or individuals perceive that they have no opportunity to engage in useful pursuits and have identified themselves as failures within education, they may be tempted to design their own social structures in which they can succeed and belong. This may include a criminal fraternity.

- *Poor social role models*: Some students have not had the benefit of positive social role models and have not developed an appreciation of the potential benefits of operating within society. They may come from families or neighbourhoods where offending is a lifestyle choice and if they operate in a law abiding way they may risk social ostracism.

- *Poverty*: Poverty may increase the risk of criminal behaviour as crime may offer an exit from poverty and access to sought-after consumer goods. Poverty is again not a cause of criminal behaviour, but it may lower an individual's resolve to resist engaging in crime.

CASE STUDY

While you are in the staff room, you overhear another tutor talking about how *another of the Roberts boys* will be in his literacy class this year making it necessary to *nail everything down* when this student is around. Further the tutor thinks *the courts should just lock them all up and save everyone a lot of trouble.*

Critical thinking activity

» What are your thoughts about a member of staff expressing this view?

» What are your professional responsibilities in this situation, if any?

» What actions should/would you take, if any?

Crime management: the roles of judicial agencies

In the United Kingdom, the Home Office is the government department responsible for managing crime via a range of different judicial agencies. Crime management in the United Kingdom may loosely be divided into two sections: crime detection (this is the responsibility of the police and the security forces) and crime regulation (this is the responsibility of the courts and associated organisations, including the National Probation Service (NPS)). Students may come into contact with the judicial agencies in a number of different ways: for example, appearing in front of Magistrates as a witness, being detained by the police for questioning or working with probation after being convicted of an offence. However, as a tutor it is important you remember that contact with a judicial authority does not necessarily equate to offending. Although a student could appear in any tier of the justice system, because most cases are dealt with by the Magistracy, it is most likely they will be involved with one of the branches of the Magistrates' Courts or associated agencies.

The diagram below shows how crime detection and crime regulation bodies are connected.

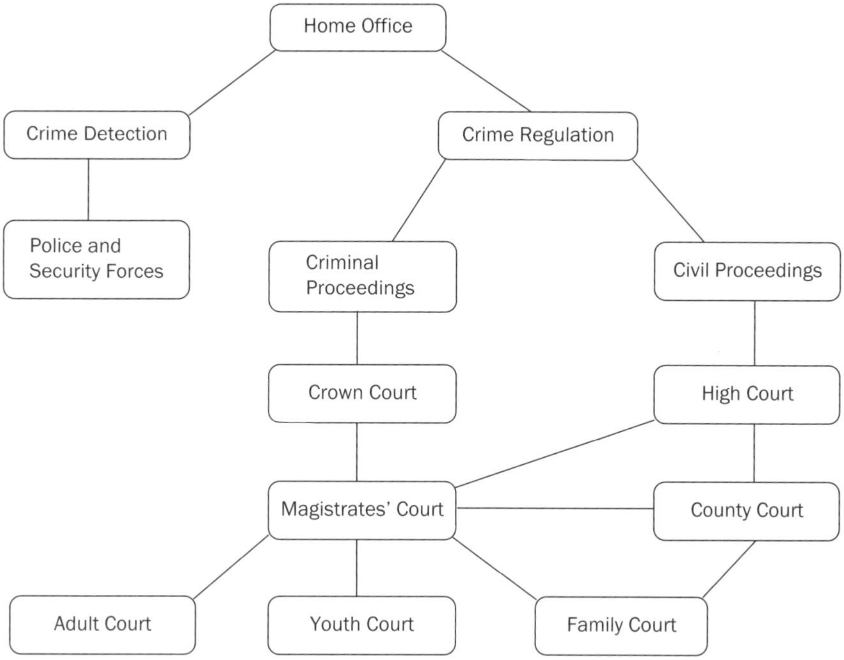

Police and security forces

Under the supervision of the Home Office, the police have authority to enforce the law and are responsible for ensuring the security and safety of the general public. As officers of Her Majesty's government, all police officers are obliged to swear an oath of allegiance to the Queen. This oath requires them to:

> well and truly serve the Queen in the office of constable, with fairness, integrity, diligence and impartiality, upholding fundamental human rights and according equal respect to all people; and .. to ... cause the peace to be kept and preserved and prevent all offences against people and property; and to ... discharge all the duties thereof faithfully according to law
>
> (Police Reform Act, 2002, Chapter 30, p 82)

In order to carry out their duties the police have the authority to arrest and detain individuals if they have good reason to believe those individuals have been involved in an offence. The police also have the power to stop and search people without necessarily arresting them. Further they are responsible for taking statements from alleged offenders and witnesses.

Crown Court

The Crown Court is one of the senior courts of England and Wales and cases are heard by a judge and jury. Crown Courts are for serious offences, such as fraud, murder and rape. Crown Courts can give lengthy community and custodial sentences including life imprisonment.

When a life imprisonment sentence is given a minimum number of years must be stated, although judges can also give 'whole life' sentences which means that the offender will never be released. Normally the defendant, that is the person who has been charged with an offence, will be represented by a barrister at the Crown Court. Because the Crown Court can impose very serious sentences, defendants are often entitled to legal aid. If legal aid is granted the costs of having a barrister are paid for from public funds.

High Court

The High Court, like the Crown Court, is one of the senior courts of England and Wales. The High Court can receive matters from the Magistrates court, the Crown Court and the County Court. The High Court can adjudicate on both criminal and civil proceedings and cases are usually heard by a single judge, although exceptionally a jury may also hear the case.

County Court

The County Court manages small civil claims up to £25,000 and very challenging family law cases. County Court cases will be heard by a single judge.

Magistrates' Court

Most cases in England and Wales are heard in the Magistrates' Courts. In a Magistrates' Court cases will either be heard by a district judge or by three magistrates. There are no juries in any branch of the Magistrates Courts. Magistrates consider a wide range of different cases varying from minor offences such as littering or dog fouling to the most serious cases such as rape and robbery. Magistrates will retain minor summary offences for sentencing but are obliged to refer the more serious offences to the Crown Court. Maximum sentencing powers in the Magistrates' Courts are six months prison (or up to 12 months, for two or more offences); fines of up to £5000; or a range of different community sentences, including curfews and unpaid work. Because Magistrates impose lesser sentences, defendants are not automatically entitled to legal aid. The Magistrates' Courts are split into three separate branches: Adult Courts; Youth Courts; and Family Courts.

Adult Court

Adults are all people aged 18 and over, and offences committed by adults are heard in this court. Youths may also appear in the Magistrates court if they are co-accused with an adult. However, any sentence a youth receives will reflect the fact that they are a young person. The adult court is an open court and any member of the public is allowed to sit in the public gallery and watch what happens. Often defendants will have to pay for all or part of their legal representation, or if they have no money and legal aid is refused they will have to defend themselves in court.

Youth Court

Youth Courts are for young people aged between 10 and 18. The age of criminal responsibility in the United Kingdom is 10 and young people below this age are not considered capable of committing a crime. Like the Adult Court, offences charged against youths begin in the Youth Court, but more serious offences will again be transferred to the Crown Court. As a feature of their age, youths are usually treated less harshly than adults and would often receive a less severe sentence than an adult who had committed the same offence. The Youth Court is a closed court and is not open to members of the public. Reporting restrictions are also in place and even if a youth is found guilty of an offence, the press do not have the automatic right to print details of the case. Young people must be accompanied by either a parent or a guardian when they appear in the Youth Court. Youths are not automatically given legal aid and granting legal aid will depend on parental or guardian income and the nature of the charge.

Family Court

Family Courts, although a branch of the Magistrates' Courts, do not deal with criminal offences. Family courts are principally concerned with the care arrangements of children and young people and will consider issues such as who has parental responsibility of a young person up to the age of 18; adoptions; fostering arrangements; and contact arrangements for parents and other family members for a child or young person in care. Like the Youth Court, the Family Court is a closed court and is not open to the public. Magistrates can refer a matter onto the County Court if there are particularly difficult legal issues that require the expertise of a Judge.

National Probation Service

The National Probation Service (NPS) is one of the main organisations that support the courts in managing offenders. They may assist the courts in recommending relevant community orders or programmes and will supervise the offender once sentence has been passed. An assigned probation officer will meet regularly with the offender to monitor their progress and to advise the courts if there are any difficulties with the order being completed.

CASE STUDY

One of your tutor group, Tony, who has only just had his 18th birthday, asks to speak to you privately. When you meet with him he tells you that following an incident in the town centre with another group of young males he and they were arrested, taken to the police station and questioned about the event. He thinks there were about 10–14 young men involved at the time. Tony co-operated fully with the police and answered all the questions he was asked. He and his friends were then released on police bail and instructed to return to the police station in three weeks time after further enquiries had been made. He shows you the bail sheet he has been given which he has signed. Tony tells you he does not think that he has been formally charged, but he is not certain. He is not sure if his interview will be considered as an official statement, although he confirms he was asked to sign the handwritten notes made by one of the police officers who questioned him. Two police officers were present when Tony was questioned but he did not have a solicitor or any other representative with him. He tells you when he was in the police station he just wanted to *get out and go home* and he was not *really thinking straight* although he does not think he said *anything stupid*. He informs you it is the first time he has ever been arrested, but he has been stopped and questioned by the police before when he has been out with his friends. Tony lives at home with his Mum, who is a single parent since his Dad left about six years ago. Tony still sees his Dad regularly and you believe that they have a good relationship.

Tony is very worried about this event. He tells you he has been *thick* and does not know why he became involved. He realises now he should have *just walked away*. He does not want his Mum or Dad to know what has happened as he does not want to worry them with his *problems* and they *have enough on already*. However, he really does not want to go to the police station by himself when he has to return to answer his bail. He does not directly ask you to accompany him but you form the impression he is hoping you will volunteer to go with him. You can see that he has found this a sobering event and he is genuinely worried about returning to the police station alone.

Critical thinking activity

» What would/should your initial response be to Tony?

» What are your responsibilities towards Tony and his Mum and Dad?

» What are your responsibilities towards the College and other staff at the college?

» Who needs to be informed of this incident? What is the basis for your decision?

» If you offer to accompany Tony to the police station on his next visit, what are the professional implications for you?

» Would your responses be different if Tony was 16?

CASE STUDY

You are teaching a mixed group a session on basic numeracy. This is a regular timetabled session and you have had the group for about four weeks. The group is usually quite lively and vocal. While you would prefer them to be quieter, you have accommodated their behaviour and rather than seeking confrontations at every point, you are trying to work with the group to modify their behaviour. You are explaining different methods of long multiplication as you are aware this is an area where they have difficulty. One of the students, Max, is talking loudly during your explanation. Another student, Kyle, who is 19 and has a reputation for being a 'hard man' from spending time in a young offenders institute is becoming visibly annoyed by Max's behaviour. In the end Kyle tells Max to *shut the f*** up* as Kyle *wants to learn*. There is an audible silence after Kyle's pronouncement and some of the other students appear visibly shocked by this statement.

Critical thinking activity

» *What would/should your immediate response be to this incident?*

» *What are your responsibilities towards Kyle, Max and the rest of the class?*

» *What would you say to Kyle, Max and other class members?*

» *As Kyle has demonstrated pro-learning behaviour, would it be acceptable to ignore his inappropriate use of language?*

» *Who needs to be informed of this event? Why?*

» *If Kyle was under the supervision of Probation, is this the sort of event you would report to them?*

» *Would your actions be influenced if you knew Kyle was serving the last four months of a custodial sentence on licence in the community?*

Discussion: having a chance

Law and order, like education and the NHS, are popular discussion topics for many people including college staff and students. While tutors may have views on what should happen to offenders, they also have professional responsibilities. FE promotes itself as a second chance sector, a place where the past does not necessarily influence the present, a place where those wishing to make a change are allowed the opportunity to do so. Although the Roberts boys, whom we heard the staff member refer to earlier, may have developed a poor reputation, FE is predicated on the belief that change can and does happen. Indeed, some students are critically aware that they have a difficult past and may purposely choose to leave a certain location to attend a college which is some distance away from their home to help them start afresh. Colleges are meant to be places which enable and help students realise their aspirations, not condemn them for their history. Equally it is important to remember that the primary business of FE is education, not policing. Tutors who pre-judge students based on their family associations or past, need to be reminded that colleges are centres of opportunity, not detention. Depending on your position within the college whether and how you challenge other tutors who glibly make stereotypical assumptions may vary. If you are a senior member of staff or feel sufficiently confident, you may choose to address these state-ments outright and point out how damaging such views can be for students' life chances; if you feel less confident you may elect to have a quiet conversation with the staff member concerned; or if you feel you lack status or confidence, you could refer the matter on to the staff member's line manager.

Role conflict

Tutors have multiple roles in colleges and sometimes students make requests outside of the norm. Accompanying a student to answer police bail is such a request. Tony is an adult. It is perfectly reasonable to expect him to attend the police station by himself. Yet Tony has sought you out to tell you about his difficulties. He has also let you know that he does not want to worry his family. As Tony is an adult, your relationship is with him and not with his family. However, this is a difficult situation as his mother and father may at some later time ask why you decided not to inform them of these circumstances. After all, he is not your son. In this situation there is no straightforward right or wrong. Morally you may feel you want to go with Tony to the police station to offer him some support, but you may also feel that you want to notify his parents. In the first instance, it would be prudent to inform your line manager of this situation and seek their advice before agreeing to do anything. If your line manager says you can accompany Tony, then you may want to make a condition that Tony tells his parents what has happened. This way Tony still controls how and when information is released to his family. However, you have no guarantee he will keep his end of the bargain. If Tony was 16 and still a minor, you would be obliged to inform his family of his dealings with the police. However, you could still accompany Tony to the police station to offer support with the consent of one of his parents.

Doing the right thing wrong

The classroom situation with Kyle and Max is an interesting one. On one level Kyle has shown positive pro-education behaviour and demonstrated his willingness to learn. This is good. However, the way in which he has expressed his support is questionable. Max may be causing difficulty in the class, but he should not be threatened or intimidated. You will have to deal with both Kyle's and Max's inappropriate behaviour. In the first instance, your priority is to restore order in the classroom. As the class has already quietened down, you may wish to capitalise on this and swiftly refocus everyone's attention on the numeracy problem being discussed. This will help to diffuse the situation by not focussing on the negative impact of Kyle's outburst and also allows you a chance to consider what you will say to Kyle and Max at the end of the session. It would be best to speak to the two students separately, as to bring them together straight after the incident could be explosive. As Max had talked repeatedly during your explanation, it would be sensible to deal with his behaviour first; you can then approach Kyle at a later point but before the next lesson, to remind him that you are the tutor and that it is your role to manage other students' behaviour. It is not usual to report individual events to the judiciary services like probation, but if this were a pattern of behaviour, you may consider involving Kyle's probation officer.

Range of sentencing options

Once an adult or a young person has been convicted of a crime, the Magistrates or Judge will need to decide what sentence should be given. There are defined sentencing guidelines in the United Kingdom and Magistrates and Judges are expected to impose a sentence that conforms to these guidelines unless they have exceptional reasons for doing otherwise. Sentences given by the courts have the following main objectives:

- To punish the offender for their crime;
- To protect the public from risk of further offending;
- To rehabilitate the offender so that they will discontinue their criminal activities;
- To make reparations to the victims of crime.

The final sentence given by the court will reflect the weighting given to each of these objectives.

As most cases are heard within the Magistrates courts, only the sentences passed by Magistrates will be considered in this section.

Custodial sentences

Custody is reserved for the most serious crimes and is the most severe penalty Magistrates can give. Magistrates will impose a prison sentence when the offence is so serious that only a custodial sentence reflects the gravity of the offence and there is not sufficient offender mitigation to suspend the sentence. In these circumstances, the offender will be taken to an appropriate venue, such as a prison, young offender institution or a secure unit for offenders with mental health problems, to serve their sentence. Magistrates will usually order pre-sentence reports before passing a custodial sentence. While waiting for reports to be prepared the defendant may be remanded into custody or released on bail into the community.

Suspended custodial sentences

A suspended sentence may be given when the Magistrates have determined that the crime is so serious that only a custodial sentence can be given for the offence, but because of the particular circumstances of the offender, the sentence can be suspended for between six months to two years. During the suspended period, the offender is allowed to remain at liberty in the community provided they complete certain requirements. Failure to complete any of the requirements imposed by the Magistrates may result in the offender being taken into immediate custody to serve the remaining period of their sentence.

Fines

Fines are imposed as a punishment for the offence, and the size of the fine will reflect both the seriousness of the crime and the offender's ability to pay. Fines may be paid either as a single payment or in monthly or weekly instalments. If the offender is receiving benefit, the court may order the fine should be deducted directly from the offender's benefit. Fines should normally be paid off within 12 months.

Community sentences

Community sentences can be given by Magistrates provided the offence has not crossed the custody threshold and the offender does not have a lengthy record. Community sentences are designed to both punish the offender and to assist them to change their behaviour so they can lead a law-abiding lifestyle and are often imposed with specific requirements. Community sentences are monitored by the NPS who may be responsible for delivering some of the specified requirements of the sentence. Requirements may also be imposed for suspended custodial sentences and could include the following:

- *Unpaid work*: Magistrates can order the defendant to complete from 40 to 300 hours of unpaid work. 300 hours is the most severe penalty that can be imposed and is at very borderline of custody. Unpaid work can include tasks such as canal cleaning or graffiti removal and could be accompanied by an additional condition to attend certain classes, particularly if the task requires new skills. Unpaid work is supervised by the NPS.

- *Programmes*: Programmes are managed by the NPS and are designed to help the offender reform and to identify how they can change their behaviour. Examples of programmes include drink driving courses; understanding the impact and cycle of domestic abuse; developing thinking skills and understanding of the consequences of their actions.

- *Education*: Many offenders have low literacy or numeracy levels and their low academic attainment may have contributed to their offending. In these circumstances as a part of their sentence offenders may be required to complete basic skills classes. The NPS would signpost the offender to relevant classes but would not normally take responsibility for teaching these sessions. Once enrolled on a course, academically the offender would be the responsibility of the education provider like any other student.

- *Curfews:* Curfews require the offender to be at a named location, usually their home address, at certain times. Curfews are designed to break the cycle of offending or to reduce the opportunity to commit offences. Curfews are often imposed at night to prevent night-time break-ins, or may be imposed in two-hour daytime blocks to interrupt opportunities for shop theft. Curfews are supervised by different agencies including the NPS and the police.

- *Exclusions:* Exclusions may be imposed if offending is associated with a particular area or people. This might include being banned from shopping centres if shop theft is the key concern; or from meeting with named others if the offence has been committed as part of a group action.

- *Electronic Monitoring (also known as tagging):* Tagging can be a useful alternative to custody and enables the movements of an offender to be tracked. An offender may also be tagged when they are released from prison, or in conjunction with another requirement such as a curfew. Tags are worn at all times and cannot easily be removed. Anyone who attempts to remove their tag may be found guilty of committing a further offence. Tags enable the offender to remain within the community and continue with family life, remain in employment and other legitimate pursuits. Unfortunately in some sections of the community tags have become 'badges of honour' and are seen as rite of passage into further offending. Tagging is usually managed by the NPS and the police.

Other orders and requirements

Magistrates are empowered to impose other orders and requirements. Orders are designed to specifically prevent certain types of offending and additional requirements are usually imposed in addition to the principal sentence. Common orders and requirements include the following.

- *Anti-Social Behaviour Orders (ASBOs):* ASBOs are prohibition orders and prevent an individual from carrying out certain actions associated with their offending. This may include non-association with named people or not visiting certain places.

- *Bind-overs:* Bind-overs are imposed when there is a risk of similar offences being committed in the short-term future. Bind-overs are for a specified period of time, usually between 6 to 12 months and for an identified sum of money. The offender must promise to be of good behaviour and to keep the peace. If the offender breaks the terms of the bind-over they can be ordered to pay the identified sum to the court and can be re-sentenced for the original offence.

- *Compensation:* Magistrates must *always* consider compensation where the victim has suffered either loss or harm to their person or property. Compensation is a priority debt and will be paid before any fine or court costs. Compensation is awarded in addition to the main sentence.

- *Court costs:* The prosecution will usually apply for, and Magistrates must consider awarding, court costs for all or part of the cost of bringing a case to court. Court costs are payable in addition to the principal penalty given.

CASE STUDY

At the end of a long and challenging year, one of your groups announces five minutes before the end of the lesson that they have *something for you*. One of the students then leaves the room and comes back in with a box which they say is a gift. The group insists you open the box and see what your gift is. You duly do so. On opening the box, you pull out an expensive wireless kindle. The group informs you they *hope you like it* because they know *you like reading*. You are very surprised and you are also very concerned as you suspect that even if the group had a collection for you they could not afford such a gift and, knowing something of their previous history, you think this gift may have been stolen.

Critical thinking activity

» *How do you feel about this event? Are you flattered? Are you pleased the group no longer appear to consider reading an oddity?*

» *How would/should you respond to this situation?*

» *What support do you need to manage this situation?*

» *What are your priorities in this situation?*

» *What line of questioning, if any, would you pursue with the group? When and how would you do this?*

» *Who, if anyone, would you report this incident to? Is there anyone you are contractually obliged to report this matter?*

CASE STUDY

When working with a group of students, you mention that your car has failed its MOT and it will be expensive to fix before it can be re-tested. One of the students, Vince, informs you that he can *sort it* as he *knows people*. You ask if the people he knows are garage mechanics. He laughs and tells you they are not, but if you need a MOT he can *sort it out* and it will be a *lot cheaper than going to a garage*. The implication is that in some way either he or his associates know how to falsify MOT certificates.

Critical thinking activity

» *What is your response in this situation?*

» *What credibility would you attach to this student's claims? Would you be inclined to believe these claims or would you view them as bravado?*

» *Has Vince committed any offence at this point?*

» *Who needs to be informed of this event? Why?*

» *If, after further exploration you decide Vince is telling the truth, what would your next actions be?*

Discussion: questionable offerings

Students sometimes feel very grateful to their tutors who they see as having helped them achieve their goals in life and they wish to show their gratitude by presenting gifts. Often these gifts are legitimately obtained by everyone in the group contributing to a collection, are simply an expression of thanks and represent a positive group endorsement of your teaching. Such modest gifts should be received with grace. Some colleges may have local policies on staff gifts and may stipulate that staff can receive only 'table-top' presents; this would of course exclude envelopes with large cheques or the keys for a four-wheel-drive which would fit on a table-top.

However, gifts you suspect have been obtained through criminal activity are different. If you truly suspect a gift has been stolen, you will need to report this situation to your line manager. Although this may break the trust you have established with your group, your professional responsibilities oblige you to report suspected wrong-doing. If your line manager then decides to follow up this matter and question class members, you need to show you are supporting this decision. Pursuing such matters is extremely difficult and students often choose to close ranks and not talk. As college staff are not police officers and cannot make students talk, ultimately your line manager may have to report this event to the police and allow them to continue the investigation.

Similarly if Vince is offering what appear to be falsified documents to you, you cannot accept these. Again it would be wise to refer this matter to your line manager. If Vince's claims are bravado, you have taken appropriate action. However, it is worth noting that at this point Vince has not committed any offence and it may be sufficient for the line manager to issue Vince with a suitable warning regarding his behaviour and the likely difficulties he could find himself in if he were to pursue a criminal lifestyle. It is further worth noting that falsifying MOT documentation now is now extremely difficult as all records are held electronically. If Vince is able to provide false MOT documentation he is associating with IT-literate felons who are able to hack into DVLA computer records. Vince may simply be out of date and is fantasising about a previous time when paper records were common. However, while extremely difficult, it may be possible that Vince is associating with IT hackers and he may be able to gain counterfeit MOT certificates as he has claimed.

Chapter reflections

This chapter has considered the range and level of offending in the United Kingdom and how the lurid newspaper reports sometimes barely resemble reality. You have been invited to consider your own responses to these headlines and how you will manage student reactions. Some of the factors that may lead to offending have been identified and how these factors may either be considered an individual's personal responsibility, or could be the result of societal factors. The critical thinking tasks have asked you to consider some of the different ways that students may become involved with offending and choices you might have to make if you found yourself working with students in similar, or potentially even more challenging, situations. While society has produced a legal framework for all its citizens and colleges have produced their own rules, you will need to decide what actions you would take and how you would approach each of these different cases. This could mean asking yourself searching questions about your own professionalism and developing a clear understanding about your contractual duties to your college.

LEARNING REVIEW AUDIT

Topic	I feel confident in doing this	This is an area I will need to develop
I can describe the scope and levels of offending in the United Kingdom		
I am able to identify factors which may increase the likelihood of offending		
I can identify the range of different judicial agencies that students may come into contact with and I understand the roles of these different groups		

Topic	I feel confident in doing this	This is an area I will need to develop
I have a better understanding of the range of sentencing options available to the courts		
I have better awareness and understanding of my personal and professional responsibilities		

Taking it further

Archer, L, Hollingworth, S and Mendick, H (2010) *Urban Youth and Schooling*. Maidenhead: Open University Press.

Hayton, A (ed) (1999) *Tackling Disaffection and Social Exclusion: Education Perspectives and Policies*. London: Kogan Page Ltd.

Macdonald, R and Marsh, J (2005) *Disconnected Youth? Growing Up in Britain's Poor Neighbourhoods* Basingstoke: Palgrave MacMillan.

www.gov.uk/government/organisations/home-office The Home Office

www.nationalprobationsrevice.co.uk/page1.html National Probation Service

www.gov.uk/courts/magistrates-courts Magistrates Courts

References

Beckford, M, Cooper, D and Hall, W (2013) *UK is Violent Crime Capital of Europe.* The Daily Mail, 10 August 2013. Available at www.dailymail.co.uk/news/article-2389085/Britains-crime-hotspots-Astonishing-new-figures-identify-lawless-postcodes-country--zero-Londons-Westfield-Shopping-centres.html Accessed 19 August 2013.

Doyle, J (2012) Under-18s Commit a Quarter of All Crimes: Young Offenders Responsible for More than a Million Crimes in just One Year, *The Daily Mail,* 26 May 2012. Available at www.dailymail.co.uk/news/article-2150187/Under-18s-commit-quarter-crimes-Young-offenders-responsible-million-crimes-just-year Accessed 27 April 2013.

Edwards, R (2009) UK is Violent Crime Capital of Europe, *The Daily Telegraph,* 2 July 2009. Available at www.telegraph.co.uk/news/uknews/law-and-order/5712573/UK-is-violent-crime-capital-of-Europe.html Accessed 19 August 2013.

Foster, A (2005) *Realising the Potential: A Review of the Future Role of FE Colleges.* Nottingham: DfES.

Home Office (2002) *Police Reform Act 2002*. London: The Home Office.

Home Office Statistical Bulletin (2013) *Crimes Detected in England and Wales 2012–13*. London: The Home Office.

Leapman, B (2008) Violent Youth Crime Up a Third, *The Telegraph,* 20 January 2008. Available at www.telegraph.co.uk/news/uknews/1576076/Violent-youth-crime-up-a-third Accessed 27 April 2013.

Newburn, T and Shiner, M (2005) *Dealing with Disaffection: Young People, Mentoring and Social Inclusion*. Cullompton: Willan Publishing.

Prison Reform Trust (2003) *Time to Learn*. Prison Reform Trust. Available at www.prisonreformtrust. org.uk/uploads/documents/Time_to_LearnBook.pdf Accessed 19 August 2013.

Stephenson, M (2007) *Young People and Offending: Education, Youth Justice and Social Inclusion*. Cullompton: Willan Publishing.

Travis, A (2013) Crime at Its Lowest Level for 30 Years, *The Guardian,* 25 April 2013. Available at www.theguardian.com/uk/2013/apr/25/uk-crime-falls-official-figures Accessed 19 August 2013.

Victim Support (2011) *Summing Up: A Strategic Audit of the Criminal Justice System* London: Victim Support.

9 Managing gender and sexual orientation issues

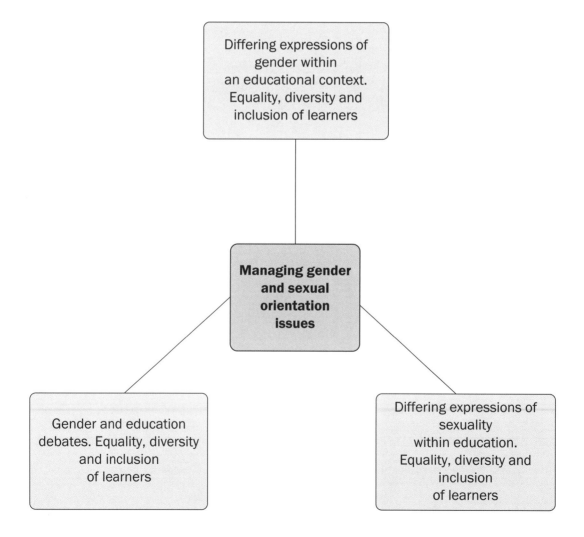

Differing expressions of gender within an educational context. Equality, diversity and inclusion of learners

Managing gender and sexual orientation issues

Gender and education debates. Equality, diversity and inclusion of learners

Differing expressions of sexuality within education. Equality, diversity and inclusion of learners

Chapter aims

In common with all areas of education, the gender debate has metamorphosed over time and other, new discussions have developed. As a tutor you need to be aware of these different issues and to understand your responsibilities in establishing a positive working environment for all students. After reading this chapter you will be able to:

*   engage, with confidence, in contemporary debates on gender and education;

*   discuss differing expressions of sexuality within education;

*   discuss questions related to the expression of gender and transgender issues;

*   recognise your individual preconceptions and prejudices;

*   apply in your own working life equality principles relating to gender and sexual orientation.

Gender and education debates

Most tutors today would not even consider the unsophisticated discussions which once dominated education and led to females being taught a different curriculum based on *their perceived biological, psychological and social differences* (ILEA, 1986, p 22) or resulted in class lists being ordered according to gender. That kind of crude sexism is rightly relegated to the past. However, gender and gender issues, albeit in contemporary guises, still manage to occupy much educational debate and still influence the educational trajectories of many students. New gender debates including 'over-achieving' girls, the emergence of a 'ladette' culture and how colleges can best support pregnant students now all demand attention from FE tutors.

Male/female achievement and engagement

For much of the twentieth century, males and females had distinctly different experiences of education. Many women and girls were *the victims of systematic discrimination from male classmates and the school system itself* (Francis, 2000, p 4), creating a *cocktail of discrimination [and] marginalisation [which] resulted in many girls failing to achieve* (Peart, 2009, p 24) or to perform at the same level as their male peers. However, this trend has not continued. Soon after GCSEs were introduced at the end of the 1980s, it became apparent that girls were outperforming their male peers and girls *now get better GCSE grades* (Brettingham, 2007) than their male counterparts. This attainment gap has stabilised *at around 10 percentage points difference* (Eurydice, 2010, p 5) and there has been *little variation since 1995* (ibid). This phenomenon, which has been presented *simplistically as a role reversal* (Peart, 2009, p 24) has caused significant concern in education and has resulted in a number of positive action strategies designed to support young males. These projects have included the following.

- Raising Boys' Achievements – a four year project commissioned by the DfES (2000–04) which explored pedagogic, individual, organisational and socio-cultural approaches and attempted *to create an environment for learning* (Younger et al., 2005, p 9) for underachieving boys in schools;

- Boys into Books – a joint DCSF and School Library Association (SLA) initiative (2007–08). This project was designed to provide information about books which would be particularly attractive to males and thus encourage them to read more. Although this project is no longer active many school libraries revised their stock to include more 'boy-friendly' titles;

- The Gender Agenda – a DCSF initiative (2008–09) established to *investigate, identify and disseminate practical ideas for improving the learning, motivation, involvement and attainment of underperforming groups of boys and girls* (DCSF, 2009, p 3).

However, despite significant intervention to raise males' achievement levels, women and girls are continuing to *'outperform' boys from the early years through to postgraduate qualifications* (Benn, 2014, online). As a result, it is likely that this particular issue will continue to occupy tutors' and educationalists' thoughts and efforts until both genders achieve an agreed acceptable level of attainment.

A further concern for education is the observable skewing of subject choice between males and females. This, in part, can be traced to the advice given to students. For much of the twentieth century, girls and women were routinely *persuaded, subtly and openly, that traditionally masculine subjects such as the 'hard' sciences and maths were 'not for them'* (Francis, 2000, p 5) which resulted in them studying more arts-based subjects. Indeed, during the 1900s when single-sex education was common, girls and boys studied distinctly different curricula based on their gender. This distortion in subject preference has continued into the twenty-first century and even when girls are allowed to choose their subjects, as they can when they transfer to FE, they *appear largely to revert to traditional choices ... tending to choose arts/humanities* (ibid, p 8). This difference is also apparent in vocational subjects where girls and women dominate subjects like childcare, hairdressing and beauty therapy, while other vocations such as automotive trades, plumbing and decorating are almost exclusively male. This raises significant questions for subject tutors and advice and guidance teams in FE.

Critical thinking activity

» *Within your work place, do you know how to access data on student achievement? Do you know who you should ask for this information?*

» *What is the gender distribution of achievement in your college?*

» *Specifically within your individual department/subject area, what is the gender distribution of attainment?*

» *If there is a difference in attainment, have any positive action intervention strategies been explored to address this imbalance?*

»   *What are the attitudes of your colleagues' to students choosing to study non-traditional subjects?*

»   *What are students' attitudes to their peers studying non-traditional subjects?*

»   *Does your work place have any specific support mechanisms to encourage greater participation in non-traditional areas for males and females?*

Discussion: gender and achievement

Ofsted requires colleges to analyse their achievement data using a number of different equality indicators. Consequently, it should be easy to find out the achievement levels of males and females by subject. However, not all colleges have efficient data management systems. If this describes your college, this deficit needs to be an institutional imperative. Unless colleges have robust data management processes, they cannot hope to identify difficulties and therefore would be unable to plan to rectify potential problems. Colleges should be using their data to drive improvements for all students.

If data shows there is a gender imbalance in achievement, this needs to be investigated and the following questions must be answered:

•   What is happening in curriculum areas with a disparity in achievement to create this skewing of data?

•   What action should or could the college consider to address this concern?

•   What support systems could help the college in this area?

National organisations such as the Equalities Unit and local groups based in universities or councils are often available to work with colleges to develop action plans to address attainment differences. There may also be other local groups or charities who would be willing to work alongside the college to support the college's development.

Student and staff attitudes are important as they can influence learners' opportunities to achieve. No staff member should be presenting gender-negative attitudes regarding either student achievement or subject choice. If staff are displaying such attitudes at the very least these must be challenged and it may be necessary to provide bespoke staff training. In extreme cases, it may be necessary to take disciplinary action. If students show negative attitudes these too must be challenged. Colleges should consider working with the students' union to explore whether joint staff/student college-wide work can be completed.

CASE STUDY

Read the following case study which describes Eileen's feelings about the career choice her daughter, Marie, has made.

I have always wanted the best for Marie, my only child. I had to leave school early. I wasn't good at exams and there was no way my family could support me to continue in education. I did not want my daughter to have the same experience I had and I have always encouraged her to think of her future. She isn't very academic, but she tries hard and has been predicted mostly Cs with the odd B or D for her GCSEs which she will take this summer. She's a practical girl and tells me her favourite subject is design/technology. I don't really understand what she does in this subject but it seems a mixture of cooking and other practical subjects.

She hasn't really enjoyed school and I know see she would like to try something different at 16 when she leaves, so I was in favour of her going to the local college to see what they could offer. I purposely chose to stay away as I want her to feel she can make decisions about her own future. But, I simply could not believe what she came back and told me. She said 'for a laugh' she had talked to this male teacher about doing an apprenticeship in furniture making. He even had a girl with him who was currently on the course. He told her it was important that other women understood furniture making wasn't just for men. This girl told Marie they do all sorts like furniture polishing, restoring and making small items such as bookshelves. She told Marie she was working with a small firm and attends college once a week to do theory work. This girl said it was great being an apprentice, they pay you, you can study and you only have to go to college for one day a week. She told Marie it was the best of both worlds – work and study. I have tried to talk sense to Marie and told her if she does this, she will be the only girl and she will hate it. She'll never find a job and it will just be a complete waste of time. She says she doesn't care what I think, it's her life and this is what she wants to do. I am going to go to the college, find that teacher, and tell him he must speak to Marie and let her know she is making a big mistake. I'm not saying girls can't do furniture making, just not my daughter.

Critical thinking activity

» *What are your views on Marie's decision?*

» *How accurate are Eileen's impressions of modern-day employment and training routes?*

» *In your view, has the male FE tutor behaved inappropriately in any way?*

» *What would you do if an irate parent visited to complain about the information you had given to their child? Would your responses be different if Marie was over 18?*

Discussion: career choices

Many parents agonise over their children's career choices. Eileen is no different to most parents in wanting the best for her daughter. However, in many regards Eileen is hostage to her own life experiences. Women may not have chosen furniture making or other traditional forms of male employment when Eileen was at school. However, Eileen's school career is a generation away. Since that time there have been seismic changes in the world of work. These changes have been accelerated by technology and many careers previously not considered by women, such as engineering, can now be accessed. Eileen is woefully out of date.

The FE lecturer has behaved entirely appropriately. He has been asked to attend the college event to promote his course and he has fulfilled this brief. It appears that he may have also been asked to undertake positive action marketing and encourage more females to consider furniture making. Having a female apprentice with him lends credence to this suggestion. However, Eileen sounds very angry and wants to speak to someone. If Eileen contacts the college to discuss the career advice Marie has been given, it is important she is given an appointment so she can air her concerns. At 16 Marie is still a minor and although she may wish to assume adult responsibilities, her mother is still responsible for her and if Eileen wishes to discuss her daughter's choices she should be given this opportunity. It is not for the college to apologise for their actions, rather it is to provide Eileen with more detailed information so she can understand the rationale behind the tutor's advice. In the end though, it will be Marie studying at college, not Eileen, and the college needs to try and work with both Marie and her mother so that an amicable and positive choice can be agreed. If Marie was 18 or over the college would have no obligation to speak to Eileen as Marie would be an adult. However, as a matter of courtesy, most colleges would agree to speak with a student's parent.

'Ladettes'

All political parties agree that they want to see young people achieving well in education so that they can progress into relevant employment and make a meaningful contribution to the nation. This is seen as vital for economic well-being and to enable the United Kingdom to become *a world leader* (Leitch, 2006, p 55). As part of the national strategy to achieve this ambition, in 2007 the government set out legislative changes to raise the participation age for all young people so that by *2015 all 18 year olds [would] be... either in education, training or work* (Peart and Atkins, 2011, p 82). Specifically, young people would be expected to follow one of the three options below:

- *Full time study in a school, college or with a training provider;*
- *Full time work or volunteering combined with part time education or training;*
- *An apprenticeship*

(DfE, online)

A result of this change, coupled with rising youth unemployment, has meant that increasing numbers of young people who would have previously elected to end their formal education, have been obliged to continue their studies in FE. Some of these students form part of a new group of female learners: 'ladettes'.

'Ladettes' is a term coined by the media to describe girls or women who adopt more masculine characteristics such as being boisterous or loud. Traditionally, girls and women have been presented as education-compliant students who, with little or no intervention, could be expected to perform *well on their own* (Francis, 2010, p 21). Simply put, girls have been expected to conform to conventional gender stereotypes of being co-operative, hard-working model students. However, more recently, colleges and schools have had to manage increasing numbers of *disruptive ... mildly aggressive* (Jackson, 2006, p 12) ladettes, more concerned with gaining the positive endorsement of their peers than engaging in academic work. Further, to retain status amongst their peers, ladettes need to overtly reject *'swotty' femininities* (ibid, p 15) and present an *uncool to work* (ibid, p 74) attitude. This raises concerns for both FE tutors and for the young women involved alike.

For those young women who have left school without achieving the expected benchmark in attainment of five GCSEs graded A*-C including Maths and English, adopting ladette behaviour with its inherent *public avoidance of academic work* (ibid, 29) hinders further progression. These young women therefore put themselves at risk of repeating the academic failure they experienced at school. Further, in challenging conventional presentations of female behaviour, ladettes may alienate some teaching staff who would either consciously or unconsciously, expect or seek greater co-operation from female students. Whereas a degree of high-spirited behaviour from male students may be tolerated as simply 'boys will be boys', *similar behaviours by girls are usually regarded very differently* (ibid, p 21) and generally female students are still expected to adhere to accepted *normative models of femininity* (ibid, p 22). Although such attitudes represent unacceptable gender-based dual standards, ladettes also unwittingly contribute to their own academic problems: they prevent themselves from achieving by assuming an anti-work position and they may distance themselves from the tutors who could help them to achieve their academic goals.

Critical thinking activity

» *What are your expectations of female students attending FE? Are you aware of any changes in female learners' behaviour?*

» *What is your attitude towards male and female students? Are your expectations influenced by a student's gender? Do you make allowances or assumptions based on gender? Have you ever asked the students their views on your behaviour and attitudes towards male and female learners? If you have not sought student views, why is this?*

» *What is your attitude to students who do not conform to traditional gender stereotypes?*

Discussion: 'ladettes'

'Ladettes' are not a coherent group. Membership is transient and elective. 'Ladettes', like 'gangstas', 'rude-boys' and 'chavs' are pejorative terms to describe a less than desirable population. You will be unable to find any statistics relating to this group, so it is impossible to know the size of this population. They exist in individual perception only. However, it is likely that you and other staff members will have formed a personal assessment of the prevalence of this group.

'Ladettes' remain an elusive group as they will be perceived in different ways. What one staff member may be prepared to dismiss as youthful exuberance, another may find deeply upsetting. You will become aware of these different perceptions in the way staff choose to talk about young women, sometimes evoking the spirit of a halcyon past inhabited by 'nice young women with good manners' – a past that probably never existed.

It is difficult not to be influenced by stereotypes or our individualised expectations of behaviour, but when these stereotypes create disparity in treatment, it is a problem. There is not an expected form of behaviour that is right for young women and inappropriate for young men. There is only an accepted form of behaviour which should be expected for both genders in college. It is your professional responsibility not to be influenced by stereotypes and to focus only on the actual behaviours you observe rather than imposing a gender-specific filter

Supporting students who are pregnant and parents during maternity

Pregnancy and maternity represent two further characteristics protected as part of the 2010 Equalities Act. Natural pregnancy is possible for females once they become sexually mature and start ovulating. This can be as young as ten years old and continues until women pass the menopause. It is also possible for women who have passed the menopause to become pregnant through in vitro fertilisation (IVF) and egg donation, although this is not usual. Consequently, most women who attend college are in the age range of women who could become pregnant. As this represents a sizeable population, colleges need to consider how they will support their female students during pregnancy and afterwards during maternity.

Public reactions to pregnancy are likely to be influenced by the age of the woman who is pregnant. Teenage pregnancies and more mature pregnancies produce different public responses. Teenage pregnancies tend to

> *create discomfort and wariness ... in the past ... such young women have been ushered quickly out of sight and out of mind. There has been, until quite recently no clear expectation for education to continue*

> > (Vincent, 2011, p 1)

However, within an FE context it is very possible there may be a number of teenage and mature women who have a pregnancy. Tutors will need to work with these students and to support them to manage the demands created by pregnancy. The Equalities Challenge Unit has produced guidance on how to support students during pregnancy and maternity and advise pregnant students and nursing mothers may need the following considerations:

- *The opportunity for regular rest breaks;*
- *Toilet breaks as required;*
- *Comfortable or supportive chairs;*
- *Consideration of assessment deadlines;*
- *Alternative assessment methods if pregnancy or maternity prohibits taking a certain type of assessment;*

- *The opportunity to resit if the pregnancy or maternity results in missing an assessment;*
- *Consideration of an extension for submitting coursework.*

(Adapted from Equalities Challenge Unit, 2010, p 16)

CASE STUDY

Leanne originally attended Fair Hills FE College for two full days each week as part of an IFP programme when she studied a level 1 childcare course which included an on-site work experience component in the college creche. She also attended functional skills sessions in literacy and numeracy. She was taken to and from college on the school minibus. At this time, there were no particular features to Leanne's college career. When Leanne finished school she enrolled on a full-time level 2 childcare course and GCSEs in maths and English. Unknown to the college staff when Leanne began her course in September, she was three months pregnant. As a result of her pregnancy Leanne had to break her studies and did not finish her childcare course or her GCSEs. Leanne gave birth to her son slightly prematurely at 36 weeks. She returned to college the following September to resume her studies and put her son, Tyler, into the college creche.

Since her return to college, Leanne has developed a reputation for being difficult. Numbers of tutors have complained that she frequently arrives late, disrupts lessons on her arrival and is uncooperative and surly. She grumbles that the course is *boring* because she has done the work before. She claims she needs to leave sessions before they have finished so she can *check on Tyler* and sometimes does not return. She has failed to submit a number of assignment tasks and when asked why she has not given in her work, she replies that she was *up all night with Tyler and could not do the work.*

Critical thinking task

» *What are your feelings about Leanne's behaviour?*

» *What should the college do, if anything, to accommodate Leanne's needs?*

Discussion: pregnancy and maternity

Leanne presents an interesting case study and as a teenager is a member of a group of national concern, as the United Kingdom has one of the highest incidences of teenage pregnancies. Colleges welcome parent students. They can often bring a different and valuable perspective to learning and most colleges now offer nursery or creche facilities to allow parents to continue their studies.

The college has appropriately provided nursery care for Leanne's child. The nursery will be staffed by qualified childcare workers. If Tyler was born prematurely and had health problems he would not have been accepted into the nursery unless they could provide the necessary care. It is understandable that as a new parent Leanne has concerns about her child but to leave the lesson early and not to return is not acceptable. Leanne will have, in common to other students, agreed to a code of conduct while at college. Her current behaviour seems contrary to that code.

It is possible though that Leanne has returned to college without fully considering the implications of studying and having a young child. It would have been helpful if Leanne could have been given a 'return to study' interview. This interview could have supported Leanne to plan how to manage being a parent and study so Leanne could meet her academic obligations. As Leanne completed a significant portion of the course before she had to break her studies, she may well have completed some of the tasks, and it is not surprising that she is finding some work 'boring'. Could the college acknowledge Leanne's earlier participation and excuse her attendance from some sessions, giving her alternative independent work to complete? At this stage it appears there has been a breakdown regarding Leanne's engagement with college work. This needs to be properly explored. Rather than immediately resorting to punitive sanctions, Leanne needs to meet with a staff member (possibly her personal tutor or a college counsellor) to try and plan a way forward that will be acceptable to both the college and Leanne. This could mean offering a modified timetable or could involve a further suspension of studies.

Differing expressions of sexuality

In the United Kingdom, sex and sexuality are simultaneously hidden and open discussion topics. In the public arena, these themes still form the basis of much material for popular humour; yet in daily life, our intimate relationships and to whom we are attracted, remain subjects only discussed with close friends or medical practitioners. Our sexuality forms one of the pillars of our identity and informs how we see ourselves and how others view us. It is a live topic in society and colleges alike, and whether someone is gay or straight is the subject of much casual gossip.

Heterosexuality

Heterosexuality is often depicted as the dominant, unchallenged, natural expression of sexuality. It is portrayed as being

> *as old as procreation, as ancient as the fallen lust of Eve and Adam, as eternal as the sex and gender difference of that first lady and initial gentleman. Heterosexuality, we imagine, is essential, unchanging, ahistorical*
>
> (Katz, 2007, p 13)

As well as being endorsed as the accepted and expected sexuality of all individuals, heterosexuality gains further credence through popular science and is presented as a biological necessity enforced by the need to *procreate or perish* (ibid, p 14). In education the biological imperative for heterosexuality is further reinforced though science curricula and the way human reproduction is taught, when usually only male/female sex is considered. However, there are now other options for conception and pregnancy, providing the possibility for same-sex couples or single gay and lesbian individuals to become parents. Gay males can locate an egg donor and use their own sperm to fertilise the egg which can then be carried by the egg donor or can be implanted into a surrogate mother. Similarly, lesbians can find a suitable sperm donor and arrange to be inseminated. Some of these processes may require the support of medical services and not all procedures are legal or readily accessible in all countries, but it is important to recognise there are now other ways to become a parent that do not rely on heterosexual union.

Heterosexuality is also promoted by many religions, including *dominant Christian discourse* (Seidler, 2010, p 102) which encourages gender-specific behaviours where males are *taught to ... pursue* (Connell, 2010, p 94) females for the purposes of forming relationships and raising families. Some Christian fundamentalists also argue *it is sinful to involve yourself in homosexual behaviours* (ibid), claiming homosexuality is expressly prohibited in the Bible, quoting Leviticus chapter 18, verse 22, which states *thou shall not lie with mankind as with womankind* as their justification. However, not all Christians adopt such an anti-gay attitude and notably the current head of the Catholic Church, Pope Francis, has signalled a more accepting position towards homosexuality stating in public interview, *if someone is gay, who am I to judge?* (Jones, 2013, online).

The 2010 Equalities Act expressly broadens the range of sexualities protected by law. Heterosexuality is one form of legally accepted sexuality among others. In law heterosexuality is not hierarchically superior or 'more natural' than other forms of sexuality.

Homosexuality

Homosexuality and bi-sexuality are also recognised in the Equalities Act, thus formalising the rights of lesbian, gay and bi-sexual people. The prevalence of same-sex attraction or relationships cannot be accurately estimated for a number of reasons including the following.

- Sexual attraction is not fixed and changes over time with many people confirming that at some stage in their lives they have had a same-sex relationship (Dickson, Paul and Herbison, 2003; Sell, Wells and Wypij, 1995).

- Cultural norms may mean it is difficult for individuals to declare if they are attracted to someone of the same sex (Hall, 2003).

- Some individuals may struggle to recognise and accept their personal sexuality (Jagose, 2005).

- Not all societies recognise the rights of lesbian and gay people. Notably, the Isle of Man (a UK Crown dependency) has not adopted the 2010 Equalities Act in its entirety and *has not repealed laws that specifically criminalise sexual acts between men* (Johnson, 2012: online). Thus declaring some forms of sexual activity in some locations could result in prosecution or worse.

It is likely that there will be a population of gay, lesbian, bisexual and transgender students in most colleges. In response to this, many colleges have now established specific interest groups for these students.

In common with other groups that have experienced repeated discrimination, there is a well-developed vocabulary of *derogatory terms like 'queen', 'queer', 'pansy' and 'homo'* (Glover and Kaplan, 2005, p 93) to describe gay people. More recent insults can be found on urbandictionary.com. As distasteful as it may be, it is important that FE tutors are able to recognise contemporary insults. Only by familiarising themselves with this language will they be able to challenge these terms if they are used by students or staff.

Critical thinking activity

» *What is your attitude towards different forms of sexuality?*

» *In your college, is the sexual orientation of students or staff openly discussed? If it is, how would you describe the nature of these discussions?*

» *What interest or support groups are in your college for lesbian, gay, bisexual and transgender students and staff?*

Discussion: differing sexualities

Once students have been accepted onto a course, certain questions are immaterial. A student's individual chosen sexuality is one such question and your responsibility as a tutor is to support all students to achieve. However, sexuality remains a popular discussion topic for students and staff. As a staff member you will be excluded from most student conversations of this nature. However, should you become aware, or should it be reported to you that students or staff are engaging in hostile or cruel conversations, regarding an individual's sexuality, you would be obliged to take some action. This action would vary according to the nature of the event and may simply involve you reporting this situation to your line manager, but it could include an investigation which may ultimately result in a disciplinary. Most colleges now have LGBT (lesbian, gay, bi-sexual, transgender) groups and it would be a good idea to seek the advice of this group in managing incidents of this nature.

Differing expressions of gender

In the 2010 Equalities Act, gender describes whether you are a male or a female according to your genetic construction. Using this description all people with two X chromosomes are women, while those who have one X and one Y chromosome are male. The Act protects the rights of men and women and also the rights of those who have chosen to transition from their biological birth sex to the opposite gender. Gender is much more than simple genetics and also describes *social and cultural aspects of sexual difference* (Glover and Kaplan, 2005, p xix), together with an idealised construction of masculinity and femininity where males and females are ascribed defined characteristics. Our gender is an essential feature of our identity, beginning *with the knowledge and awareness, whether conscious or unconscious, that one belongs to one sex and not the other* (Stoller, 1968, p 10) and we instinctively understand whether we are male or female.

Within Westernised societies, gender differences are developed, supported and reinforced through complex social activities that begin at birth, as explained by Connell.

From the start [children were] identified as either female or male and put into pink and blue baby clothes respectively. Blue babies were expected to behave differently from pink babies – rougher and tougher, more demanding and vigorous. The pink babies by contrast, were expected to be more passive and compliant.

(Connell, 2010, p 94)

However, some individuals experience gender dysphoria. This is a

condition in which a person feels there is a mismatch between their biological sex and their gender identity ... some people with gender dysphoria have a strong and persistent desire to live according to their gender identity rather than their biological sex.

(NHS, online)

CASE STUDY

This case study below describes a young woman's experience of her journey to transition from a male to a female.

Frances is a transgender young woman, born a biological male. She now lives as a girl. Frances (originally Craig) recognised she was different from other males in her childhood. She preferred the company of girls and eschewed conventional boy pursuits, preferring to play with dolls. Frances, still known as Craig at the time, attended the local primary school without incident. Her preference for being with other girls was not an issue. However, when Frances transferred to secondary school, things changed. Frances was regularly bullied, called names and on occasion attacked. Frances' parents who had accepted her sexuality, complained to the school which dismissed the matter seriously even though Frances has been diagnosed with gender dysphoria. When Frances turned 14 her family decided to remove her from secondary school and contacted the local FE college to see if she could continue her education there.

Critical thinking activity

»   *What issues can you identify in this case study?*

»   *What do you think would be the reaction in your college towards transgender staff or students?*

»   *What actions should the college take in its preparation to accept Frances?*

Transgender students

Frances' case raises a number of significant issues. It is not the school or the college's place to judge the choice Frances has made. Although many people may feel that she is too young to make such a significant decision, it is not *their* decision and Frances should be given the support she needs to help her reach *her* choice. She has already been clinically diagnosed with gender dysphoria and rather than creating difficulties, education establishments should work with Frances and support her during this period. Colleges and schools most certainly should provide a safe, non-judgemental environment for all students to study.

Managing change can be challenging. We may be forced to re-evaluate situations and revisit our own fears and prejudices. Colleges do not routinely teach numbers of openly transgender students. Some of Frances' peers and staff members may find the situation unsettling and confusing and may wish to voice their prejudices. Colleges must not tolerate this behaviour. If Frances was discriminated against because she had a disability, colleges would be rightly criticised. Students who are transgender are afforded the same protections and rights as other groups by the Equalities Act. Colleges need to show clear leadership and to unequivocally state that prejudice and discrimination can have no place in education.

Chapter reflections

Most people in the United Kingdom have some sort of relationship with education. Everyone is obliged to attend school until they are at least 16 and since the participation age has been raised many more students are continuing their education in FE. FE was established as an environment where students can make choices about their education. This is both liberating and challenging. While choice can produce new outcomes such as men studying beauty therapy, it can also result in reinforcing existing stereotypes with women dominating childcare. Colleges cannot make students' choices, but colleges should provide detailed information on all options so that students can make informed decisions.

Colleges must ensure that they protect individual rights and provide appropriate services and facilities for students who may be pregnant or nursing and to recognise the range of sexual orientations that exist. Colleges should work with students and the student union to accurately assess needs and then must respond to meet that need. It is incumbent on FE tutors to ensure they understand the range of sexualities that exist and are protected by the Equalities Act. Colleges need to be environments where change is embraced and welcomed and students can learn in a fear-free atmosphere.

LEARNING REVIEW AUDIT

Topic	I feel confident in this area	This is an area I will need to develop
I am familiar with a range of debates regarding gender and education		
I am aware of the different expressions of sexuality within an educational context		
I understand some of the contemporary forms of gender oppression		

Taking it further

Adams, M et al. (eds) (2010) *Readings for Diversity and Social Justice*. London: Routledge.

Collins, P H (1991) *Black Feminist Thought: Knowledge, Consciousness, and the Politics of Empowerment*. London: Routledge.

Sullivan, A (1996) *Virtually Normal: An Argument About Homosexuality*. London: Picador.

Teich, N M (2012) *Transgender 101*. Chichester: Columbia University Press.

www.bristolfawcett.org.uk Bristol Fawcett Society: Campaigning for Gender Equality

www.genderandeducation.com Gender and Education Association

www.progressivewomen.org.uk Progressive Women

References

Benn, M (2014) The Education Gender Gap Is Bad for Girls as well as Boys, *The Guardian*, 31 January 2014. Available www.theguardian.com/commentisfree/2014/jan/31/education-gender-gap-girls-schools-university Accessed 9 February 2014.

Brettingham, M (2007) Gender Gap Yawns Wider in Schools. *Times Educational Supplement,* 6 July 2007.

Connell, R (2010) *Gender*. Cambridge: Polity Press.

DfE (online) *Raising the Participation Age.* Available at www.education.gov.uk/childrenandyoungpeople/youngpeople/participation/rpa Accessed 18 February 2014.

DCSF and SLA (2008) *Boys into Books.* Available at www.sla.org.uk/blg-minister-launches-boys-into-books-at.php Accessed 9 February 2014.

DCSF (2009) *The Gender Agenda*. Nottingham: DCSF.

Dickson, N, Paul, C and Herbison, P, Same-Sex Attraction in a Birth Cohort: Prevalence and Persistence in Early Adulthood, *Social Science and Medicine*, 56 (8): 607–15.

Eurydice at NFER (2010) *Gender Differences in Educational Outcomes.* Available at www.nfer.ac.uk/shadomx/apps/fms/fmsdownload.cfm?file_uuid=67EB886D-C29E-AD4D-00A3-6752B523AE2E&siteName=nfer Accessed 9 February 2014.

Equalities Challenge Unit (2010) *Student Pregnancy and Maternity: Implications for Higher Education Institutions*. London: Equalities Challenge Unit.

Francis, B (2000) *Boys, Girls and Achievement – Addressing the Classroom Issues*. London: Routledge.

Glover, D and Kaplan, K (2005) *Genders*. Abingdon: Routledge.

Hall, D E (2003) *Queer Theories*. Basingstoke: Palgrave Macmillan.

Inner London Education Authority (ILEA) (1986), *Girls into Mathematics*. Milton Keynes: Open University.

Jackson, C (2006) *Lads and Ladettes in School: Gender and Fear of Failure*, Maidenhead: Open University Press.

Jagose, A (2005) *Queer Theory: An Introduction*. New York: New York University Press.

Johnson, P (2012), Homosexual Offenses and Human Rights in the Isle of Man, in the *Jurist.* Available at http://jurist.org/hotline/2012/12/pau;-johnso-manx-homosexuality.php Accessed 21 February 2014.

Jones, S (2013) The Year Pope Francis Allowed Britain's Catholics to Break Cover *The Guardian,* 20 December 2013. Available at www.theguardian.com/world/2013/dec/26/pope-francis-britain-catholics Accessed 18 February 2014.

Katz, J N (2007) *The Invention of Heterosexuality*. London: The University of Chicago Press.

Leitch, S (2006) *Prosperity for All in the Global Economy – World Class Skills*. London: The Stationery Office.

NHS *Gender Dysphoria.* Available at www.nhs.uk/conditions/Gender-dysphoria/Pages/Introduction.aspx Accessed 21 February 2014.

Peart, S (2009) *The Minimum Core for Numeracy: Knowledge, Understanding and Personal Skills*. Exeter: Learning Matters.

Peart, S and Atkins, L (2011) *Teaching 14–19 Learners in the Lifelong Learning Sector*. Exeter: Learning Matters.

Seidler, V J (2010) *Embodying Identities, Culture, Differences and Social Theory*. Bristol: Polity Press.

Sell, R J, Wells, J A and Wypij, D (1995) The Prevalence of Homosexual Behavior and Attraction in the United States, the United Kingdom and France: Results of National Population-Based Samples. *Archives of Sexual Behavior*, 24 (3): 235–48.

Stoller, R J (1968) *Sex and Gender: On the Development of Masculinity and Femininity*. London: Hogarth Press.

Vincent, K (2011) *Schoolgirl Pregnancy, Motherhood and Education: Dealing with Difference*. Stoke-on-Trent: Trentham Books.

Younger, M, Warrington, M, Gray, J, Rudduck, J, McLellan, R, Bearne, E, Kershner, R and Bricheno, P (2005) *Raising Boys' Achievements*. Nottingham: DCSF.

10 Managing equality and diversity in Further Education

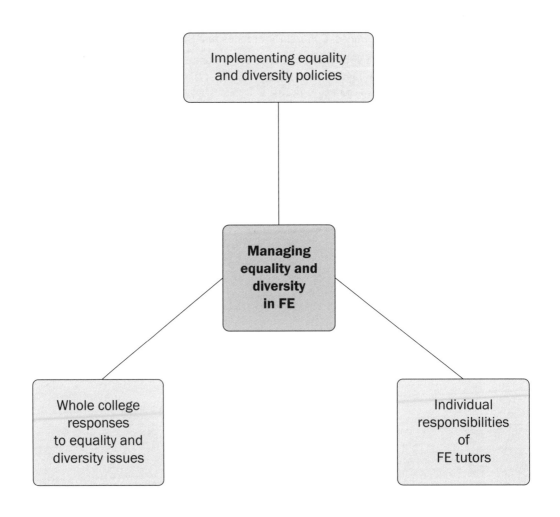

Implementing equality and diversity policies

Managing equality and diversity in FE

Whole college responses to equality and diversity issues

Individual responsibilities of FE tutors

Chapter aims

Establishing a culture which promotes equality and diversity and demonstrates it values students, staff, community partners and all other college users requires leadership. It does not happen organically. This chapter examines how colleges should respond to managing equality and diversity, what this means for senior managers, policy development in college, college lecturers and implications for the future. After reading this chapter you will be able to:

*   identify the responsibilities and roles of senior managers in developing effective equality and diversity practices;

*   understand the significance of college policy development in promoting equality;

*   detail how you, as a tutor, could be involved in policy development;

*   articulate your personal and collective responsibilities in policy implementation.

Whole college responses to equality and diversity

Discrimination is a *complex social reality* (Dadzie, 2004, p ix) and while

> *most organisations and most people now recognise the damage that [discrimination] can do to the life chances of groups and individuals. Some people and institutions find [discrimination] difficult to accommodate or even to acknowledge.*
> (Peart, 2013, p 108)

If discrimination is to be defeated, action must be taken. This begins with the Principal and Chair of Governors. To successfully challenge inequality, college managers must provide *effective leadership and management* (Bush, 2011, p 18) and *plan strategically to achieve change* (ibid, p 7). Only in this way can equality policy be translated into meaningful reality for *all* college users. To achieve this goal, managers must first identify their vision, then articulate and communicate their plans to all staff and finally implement the agreed college strategy.

Developing a vision which the whole college community can subscribe to presents a significant challenge. Each college is necessarily different from the other. The issues faced by a large, urban, general, multi-site college will be very different from those pertinent to a small, single-site, rural college which will be different again from a single-focus, specialist college. However, it is critical that colleges make the effort to develop a single unifying vision, because to not do so would risk drifting aimlessly and leaving injustices unchallenged. The challenge for college managers is how they will translate their vision *into viable day-to-day practice* (Dadzie, 2004, p ix).

Gillborn argues that prejudice *gains strength from too many quarters simply to be taught out of existence* (1995, p 2). Consequently, managers cannot expect equality in college to become a reality simply by telling staff to implement policy. This may achieve perfunctory adherence, but it does not promote ideological commitment. Real, lasting difference can only be achieved *by the efforts and energies of those committed to bringing about change* (Peart, 2013, p 109). College managers thus need to secure wide support from staff and engage all workers in meaningful dialogue so that policy can be translated into practice.

One of the first challenges in producing a whole college vision is to identify the scope of issues to be considered. Ofsted has provided a helpful overview (shown below) which lists the areas all colleges need to take into account. While this is a useful list which extends earlier notions of equality, it is important that colleges also develop contextualised responses and include important local issues.

Groups of learners to be considered in college equality policy

- *disabled learners, as defined by the Equality Act 2010, and those that have special educational needs;*
- *boys/men;*
- *girls/women;*
- *groups of learners whose prior attainment may be different from that of other groups;*
- *those who are academically more or less able;*
- *learners for whom English is an additional language;*
- *minority ethnic learners;*
- *Gypsy, Roma and Traveller learners;*
- *learners qualifying for a bursary scheme award;*
- *looked after children;*
- *lesbian, gay and bisexual learners;*
- *transgender learners;*
- *young carers;*
- *learners from low-income backgrounds;*
- *older learners;*
- *learners of different religions and beliefs;*
- *ex-offenders;*
- *women returners;*
- *teenage mothers;*
- *other vulnerable groups.*

(Ofsted, 2014, pp 42–3)

Colleges should develop practices and procedures to support the learners identified by Ofsted, and more progressive colleges may attempt to predict future needs and make provisions for learners who have not yet arrived. Although research has shown that the *quality of leadership and management is one of the most important* (Bush and Coleman, 2004, p 3) factors in achieving change, it is important to remember *management is dispersed amongst those responsible for curriculum development and student pastoral care* (ibid). Thus, college lecturers also have the capacity to *influence events* (Gillborn, 1995, p 94) and promote change.

As well as being responsible for developing policy, college managers must also discipline those who break college policy. While colleges are used to taking disciplinary action against students, equality policy applies to staff as well as students, and managers need to be prepared to take the potentially unpopular step of disciplining staff who fail to follow policy. Colleges will already have formalised disciplinary procedures in place and these should be implemented in the event of staff misconduct.

Running parallel to policy development, colleges need to provide *proper training on ... equality* (DfES, 2006, p 17). Unfortunately, as recently as 2005, Ofsted reported that in too many colleges there was *insufficient training* (2005, p 21) on equality. Ofsted's observations are significant, particularly as evolving agendas mean new training priorities continue to arise. Staff have had a considerable time to become familiar with issues associated with gender, race and disability as these were the first areas to have definitive equality legislation. However, needs change with time. In relation to race, the needs of a Somali migrant arriving in Britain today could not possibly be the same as those of a Jamaican arriving in the 1960s. Similarly there have been significant changes in gender and disability debates which require different, contemporary responses. Other, new equality priorities have also become apparent, such as working with transgender students and offenders. FE staff have a professional responsibility to remain up to date with equality discourses and to understand their impact on professional practice. Information sharing remains an important training feature and colleges might reasonably be expected to provide whole staff briefings for new, emergent issues. However, increasingly staff are expected to take responsibility for organising their own professional development and can no longer rely on their employer to manage all training. Staff need to be pro-active in this regard and to explore creative learning opportunities. This may involve working with internal colleagues, staff from other organisations, professional and voluntary sector organisations or utilising online training resources.

CASE STUDY

Sandra worked as a sociology tutor. One of the students in her group, as a result of his disability, needed to have an adapted chair. This chair was always in the classroom where Sandra taught and had a large notice attached to it which said *Please do not use this chair. Needed for a specific student. Please ensure this chair is left in this room*. Sandra had been teaching her group for eight weeks and the chair had always been in the room where it was needed. However, in the ninth week, Sandra arrived to teach and unfortunately the adapted chair was not there. Sandra asked the student to wait while she attempted to find the chair by looking in the neighbouring classes, but the chair was not in these rooms either. The student informed Sandra that he could not remain and would have to go home as he could not use a chair without adaptations. He informed Sandra he intended to make a formal complaint. Sandra asked him to give her a chance to resolve this situation and not submit a complaint at this point. The student agreed, but informed Sandra he expected her to make sure the chair was returned to the classroom. After Sandra had given the student some relevant work, he left, and Sandra then taught the rest of the class.

As Sandra knew the only staff members who routinely moved furniture were the premises staff, she decided to call at their office at the end of her teaching session. When she visited the office, she enquired about the missing chair. The premises staff were very apologetic and informed Sandra that the missing chair was their error as it had not been returned after some routine maintenance work. They were sorry for their mistake and promised that the chair would be returned that day. As she was leaving their office Sandra noticed a nude female calendar displayed on the office wall. Sandra had recently attended a briefing by the college's equalities and diversity group and had formed the impression that nude calendars were prohibited in all staff areas.

Critical thinking activity

»   *What equality issues can you identify in this case study?*

»   *What actions do you feel should Sandra take?*

»   *What could be the potential outcomes of these actions?*

»   *What are Sandra's priorities in this situation?*

»   *Does it matter if some staff display nude calendars in private office spaces?*

»   *Would your responses be different if this was a head of department's office?*

Policy development and implementation

Whole college policy development is logically the first step in promoting equality. However, colleges are not static environments, and it is more likely that staff will have a greater or lesser understanding of equality issues. Unless it is a brand new college, opening for the very first time, college managers will not be working with a blank sheet on which they can impress their vision. More realistically college managers will have to work with an existing team, some of whom will be supportive of equality action and some of whom will be resistant.

Kotter, in a model he developed in the 1990s, proposed eight stages to successfully implementing change. He identified these stages as:

1. *Create urgency*

2. *Form powerful coalitions*

3. *Create a vision for change*

4. *Communicate the vision*

5. *Remove obstacles*

6. *Create short-term wins*

7. *Build on the change*

8. *Anchor the changes in the corporate culture*

(Adapted from Kotter, 2012, pp 37–169)

Current legislation and Ofsted inspection procedures mean that all colleges should have equality policies in place. Creating urgency, the first stage of Kotter's model, therefore should not be required as equality policy is an implied institutional requirement. However, as recently as 2005 Ofsted reported that *too few [colleges] were actively and systematically instigating change to improve ... equality at the rate which might be expected* (Ofsted, 2005, p 1). Worryingly, Ofsted also commented that one of the primary barriers to successfully achieving change was the lack of *leadership of the Principal and senior managers in establishing a college-wide ethos of equality* (ibid), unfortunately suggesting *widespread institutional com-placency* (Peart, 2013, p 112). Kotter's model is helpful as it reminds colleges that if change is to be effective, a whole college sense of urgency must be created first.

College working parties are a useful tool in helping to establish the sense of urgency needed to begin the change process. Although usually commissioned by senior managers to complete a defined task within a specified time, working parties are normally open to staff working at all levels and from all areas. Working parties can therefore support building strong internal coalitions and can be tasked to progress developments. However, they must be managed carefully. The remit of the group needs to be clearly stated by managers at the outset. Such groups usually have an advisory and developmental function rather than an enforcement role. Any suggestions identified by the group would normally need to be ratified by the college management team. It is important that group members understand the limitations of their role in order to avoid later confrontations or disappointments. Additionally working parties help to promote greater democratization of decision making in colleges by providing non-teaching and teaching staff an opportunity to work collaboratively to influence developments.

Because working parties are made up of a cross-section of the college population, they support internal communication. As a result, they are ideally placed to minimise or remove potential staff resistance by explaining the vision to all staff. The effective dissemination of the vision is, in itself, an important short-term win. Depending on how long the working party will operate for, they may also be a useful in embedding new practices within college culture.

CASE STUDY

Claire, a black female lecturer, had been on the college's Managing Diversity Working Party for two terms. By agreement, the group had decided it would try to establish a LGBT (lesbian, gay, bisexual and transgender) group for college users. Claire agreed she would put up posters on college notice boards to advertise this new initiative. When she was pinning up one of the posters Yvonne an older, White, female staff member approached Claire and asked her why she was pinning up *such rubbish*. Claire explained the LGBT group was an agreed development supported by the College's Managing Diversity Working Party and the college Principal. Yvonne tutted and stated *a Christian college didn't need group like that* and was surprised *a coloured person* was supporting this plan.

Critical thinking activity

» *What immediate issues does this case study present?*

» *What can you discern about the success of communicating new equality initiatives to the wider staff team in this college?*

» *What actions should Claire take in this instance?*

» *Where should Claire go for support?*

» *What staff training needs are apparent to you in this college?*

CASE STUDY

Read the following case study about one FE tutor Andy's experience of being a member of a college working party.

To be frank, I've always been sceptical about working parties. I understand the rhetoric that those directly involved in a situation are best placed to generate solutions and are ideal messengers to disseminate ideas, but I remained doubtful. When Alex, my line manager, asked me to represent the department on the college's equality and diversity working party, my first response was 'What's in it for me? Would I be given any abatement from teaching?' Alex said 'no' but he thought it would be good for my professional development and I could be part of whole college policy development and implementation. I still wasn't convinced but I agreed.

Fortunately there weren't too many meetings, they were during the day so I did not have to stay late and to be fair there were some quite interesting debates. The Principal, who had been working closely with local Black and Asian community groups, came to speak with us at one of our meetings. She had decided the college should do more to recruit more minority ethnic staff. She had identified two posts, a photographic technician and a learning support worker, to be advertised in a different way. The college would still use its usual web advertising but rather than using the standard local press and local authority bulletin, these posts were to be heavily advertised via Black and Asian community forums. She informed us she had agreed to speak at some community meetings to try and generate interest, and had allowed a longer recruitment window to give potential applicants sufficient time to apply. The Principal had committed to this idea and it was not a topic for discussion. She was now seeking the working party's support in positively promoting this initiative. She asked us to field questions from front-line staff, explain the rationale behind the idea and if possible present this idea at internal team meetings. She did not believe that the college could fairly claim to be part of the community when its staff looked nothing like the local community. These posts were not ring-fenced solely for Black people and the most suitable applicant would be appointed, regardless of their ethnicity. Nonetheless, she had committed to take action to try and change the staffing profile. I thought it was a good idea. However, I was not at all prepared for what I can only describe as the roasting I was given when I tried to explain this idea at our department meeting. Staff who I thought I knew said things like 'Aren't White people entitled to jobs?' and 'It's just reverse racism'. I simply was not ready for such hostility and had trouble recognising colleagues who I thought supported equality action. I tried to explain this was not positive discrimination, it was positive action, it was totally legal, it did not exclude White people and I could not see what the problem was. I could tell from their faces and their comments that they were not convinced. I'm glad I joined the working party, I can see it has a real role in communicating ideas and I will not leave; but I'm still trying to get over the fact that my line manager, who asked me to join, offered me no support during the meeting.

Critical thinking activity

» *What are your immediate responses to the case study above?*

» *What does this case study tell you about the role of working parties?*

» *What are your views of working parties? Would you join one if asked? If not, why have you made this decision?*

» *What action would have you taken if you had been Andy?*

» *What is your response to the actions of Alex, the line manager?*

» *What support do you think the tutor might need after their team meeting?*

Discussion: managing challenges

Tutors are at the sharp end of policy implementation. In their daily working practices they are expected to ensure that college policy is followed. In Sandra's sociology class, the college had taken appropriate action. A student had been assessed as needing a modified chair which had been provided. When Sandra discovered the chair was missing she tried to solve the problem immediately by looking for the chair. The student reasonably registered his dissatisfaction but agreed to allow Sandra some time to try and resolve the situation. The actions of the student and the tutor both appear reasonable in the circumstances. Sandra made the best provision she could for the student at short notice, and while Sandra could be criticised for not logging this as an equality incident, her motives and actions appear well-intentioned. Indeed Sandra continued to try and find the missing chair and visited the premises staff straight after her session. The outcome of this meeting, however, was mixed.

Facing a choice

While Sandra located the chair, she also saw a calendar which she believed contravened the college's equality policy. Her primary reason for visiting the premises officers was to find the chair, a goal she successfully achieved. It was not her intention to look for transgressions of the equality policy. This was coincidental. Sandra now faced two choices: should she report the premises staff, or should she pretend she never saw the calendar, after all looking for a nude calendar was not her priority. Sandra may be worried about reporting the premises staff as she needs to work with this team and may be fearful of antagonising them. She may not even care if some staff have nude calendars in private offices. However, college premises are not private spaces and college policy applies to all staff. Sandra is at least obliged to report what she has seen to a relevant source who can then decide if further action is warranted. This might be her line manager, a senior manager with responsibility for equality or the college's equality group. Sandra should expect to be protected in this instance and should not fear her name would be passed onto the premises officers. While Sandra may not personally care about nude calendars, as an employee she is expected to promote all college policies. If a policy prohibits displaying nude calendars, this must apply to all staff including premises staff and department heads.

There are a number of pertinent issues in Claire's situation. The case study suggests that the college has been unsuccessful in communicating its vision on sexuality and gender issues to the whole staff. This is a message Claire will need to feed back to the equality working party so that the matter can be escalated to college management. While working parties can help to disseminate information, this is not their responsibility alone. In this situation, the college's management team could usefully issue a whole college bulletin or place a posting on the college's intranet regarding recent equality initiatives. Alternatively, department heads and managers could be instructed to make equality issues a standing agenda item at team meetings. Although this may not change opinions, it would at least alert staff that the college was serious about equality action. There appear to be some important, unaddressed training needs for Yvonne, the older staff member, in relation to religion, ethnicity and sexuality. She appears to have fixed views on Christianity, the Black community, and LGBT groups. Her attitude certainly appears out of date and would be viewed by many as overtly offensive. However, these training needs may only be relevant to this staff member and may not be indicative of the attitudes of other staff. Therefore, any action taken needs to be proportionate. It may be sufficient for the staff member concerned to be informed of her inappropriate language by her line manager and advised that she needs to revise how she speaks to others. She may also benefit from targeted equality training. While it is important that colleges and college managers do not shy away from tackling awkward situations, it is not always necessary to take whole college action for what could be a localised issue. To paraphrase an adage, nutcrackers, not sledgehammers, are best for cracking nuts.

Making working parties work

Andy, who was 'conscripted' onto the equalities working party, had a testing experience. As their line manager identified at the beginning, being a member of a working party can support professional development by providing personal and institutional learning opportunities. Working parties are often at the forefront of topical, sometimes controversial debate. Consequently working party members are sometimes the messengers of new, potentially unpopular, ideas. This can be very challenging for the messengers as not everyone will welcome change. However, managers need to support whole college developments. Having asked another, more junior staff member to join a working party, it is disappointing the line manager chose not to openly support the LGBT initiative in the team meeting. Because this did not happen, there now seems to be ill feeling between Andy and Alex. As both staff will need to continue to work together, it is important that they find some way of resolving their disagreement. This will be influenced by their personalities. Ideally they should arrange to meet, explore their problems and plan how they will work together in the future. If this was too difficult, they could seek mediation. If the problem became too intractable, they may need to seek the support of the Human Resources (HR) department. They could also choose to ignore the problem and pretend it never happened. However, the last option would be the least productive approach and risks leaving old wounds to fester.

Responsibilities of tutors in FE

Most contemporary FE employment contracts clearly stipulate that it is a requirement to adhere to college policy. All colleges should have an equality policy in place and therefore, by implication, all staff should support equality action. However, promoting equality is more than implementing policies. Equality is about fairness, a willingness to learn, the capacity to change and recognising that each individual has the right to be treated with respect. Equality is about establishing an ethos which values all college users and provides opportunities for everyone to contribute to the running the organisation. Implementing equality is an ideological position and essentially concerns power sharing and the increased democratization of organisations.

While governments are responsible for sector-wide initiatives and colleges translate these initiatives into policy, each tutor is the manager of their own learning environment and has individual, professional and moral responsibility to promote equality in that setting. Tutors can choose to manage autocratically and not engage with students, or can choose to share power by providing opportunities for learners to make some decisions about their studies. Working in this way may be new for some tutors and they may struggle to manage the implications of sharing authority with students.

CASE STUDY

Graham had set his group project work. At the outset of the project, Graham allowed the students to choose their own groups and who they would work with. Graham was uneasy about this situation and was worried some groups would produce very good work while other groups would barely pass. However, he had decided he was going to pass some decision-making responsibility to his class. He had informed the group that while they were working on the project they did not need to be physically based in the classroom, but they were expected to report in at the start and end of each session, and to provide regular updates on progress. Graham had scheduled four weeks for the project and the fifth week was to be used for presentations.

In week three, two of the more able groups informed Graham that they would be absent in week four as they had finished their project and could not see the point in attending. They had other course work to complete and would rather concentrate on that. Graham also noticed that one of the groups had decided to call their team 'South Side Super Studs'. When challenged about their choice of name, the group pointed out that Graham had previously proclaimed the importance of free speech in a democracy and that they were simply exercising this right.

Critical thinking activity

» *What issues does this situation raise for Graham, the group members, the rest of the class and the college?*

» *What action should Graham take at this point?*

» *What implications does this situation raise for future project work?*

CASE STUDY

Pine Trees College had recently introduced a grade restriction policy for assignments. Work submitted on or before the deadline could achieve all grades; work submitted after the deadline with good reason could also achieve all grades; late work submitted up to seven days after the submission deadline without good reason would be capped at a pass; all work submitted more than seven days late would be recorded as a fail, though tutors may provide an indicative mark to show what score students might have achieved. Under the college policy, each tutor had been given the authority to decide what they considered a good reason. Paul, one of the students in your personal tutor group, has complained to you that the college has refused to recognise that he was attending celebrations organised for L. Ron Hubbard's birthday, the founder of Scientology. He handed in his work one day late and was informed that attending Scientology events was not a good reason, therefore his work would be capped at a pass. He is particularly angry as he knows other students have given in work late at other times, for example when attending Eid celebrations. He wants to know why Islam is recognised by the college, but Scientology is not.

Critical thinking activity

»   *What are your responses to the case study above?*

»   *What is your college's position regarding religious holidays? Which religions are included? Are all religions afforded equal merit?*

»   *What is your personal view on minority religions?*

Discussion: implementing equality

Equality policy demands fairness and parity of treatment. However, while this may seem simple on one level, the actual implementation for fair, equitable treatment for all college users is extremely difficult. College policy often begins by identifying named groups whose particular needs should be considered. This is the same approach adopted by Ofsted in its most recent inspection documentation. This in itself is problematic. To try and list all groups will almost inevitably mean some groups are omitted. To cover this eventuality, Ofsted has suggested *other vulnerable groups* (Ofsted, 2014, 43) should be considered. However, in taking this action Ofsted seems to imply that other groups are not as significant as specifically named groups. The other option that could be adopted is to state that *everyone* should be treated fairly and no individual group should be identified. However, the risk of homogenising everyone into one amorphous mass means specific needs might be easily forgotten. From the outset therefore, catering for all individual needs and being seen to be fair is a demanding and almost unattainable goal. Nonetheless, simply because a task is difficult is not an excuse for colleges not to engage with this challenge. In this instance, some action, even if it is imperfect, is much better than no action at all.

Graham is wrestling with the problem of how much decision-making responsibility to give to students. In the light of his personal misgivings, it is admirable that he has attempted to work democratically at all. However, Graham is now in difficulty. It appears Graham did not stipulate the parameters of the project clearly enough at the beginning and students have attempted to exploit this lack of clarity. Graham also appears to have failed to stretch the more able students. Students will often perform at different levels. Project work should be designed so that the weaker students can achieve at least a pass, and higher achieving students are given opportunities to produce unique, distinctive solutions. This will almost inevitably mean providing access to a rich resource bank which students can use to enhance their work. Graham needs to avoid the trap of issuing 'filler' extension work to his most capable students and now needs to write a project which truly caters for the entire range of abilities. Although there are concerns with Graham's project planning, it would probably be ill advised to allow students not to attend further lessons, as Graham might face accusations of favouritism. If he has insisted that students attend for at least part of the session, he must now follow this through. One of the groups has decided to call their team a sexist name. Again, it appears Graham was not adequately clear at the outset. Naming a team is a good idea, it gives ownership and identity. However, all names must conform to college policy. Democracy has never implied a 'free-for-all' and existing policies must be adhered to. The use of sexist, or other derogatory or exclusionary language would be expressly prohibited by the college policy and this should have been explained to the groups.

Accommodating minority perspectives

The case study about Paul, who is a Scientologist, is particularly interesting. Students of all denominations and beliefs will attend colleges. College equality policies often state that religious observances of differing groups will be respected. However, while most colleges recognise major world religions, minority religions may not be accorded the same respect. Perhaps it is important to remember that Christianity, which significantly influences most UK-based colleges' annual teaching calendars, was once considered a fringe, cult religion. Perhaps other minority religions might, over time, gain such ascendancy. The student concerned is understandably irritated. From his perspective it must seem as though some religions are given more respect than others. This must be at odds with any equality policy. If you were Paul's personal tutor, you should help the student to challenge this inequity. This situation would need to be investigated and it would need to be ascertained whether other religious groups were penalised for late submission of work if attending religious events. It would be unfair to ask the student to produce documentary evidence of his attendance if other groups were not required to do so. Significant power has been given to individual tutors because they can decide what a *good reason* is. While this may be expedient for many situations, it is not always appropriate and could create considerable variation in policy interpretation. At the very least there needs to be an established appeal process so that this student can challenge whether he has been treated fairly. Religion is a deeply personal subject and how colleges accommodate religious observances continues to be a matter of debate. The 2010 Equalities Act specifically includes religion as a protected characteristic. However, when interpreting this legislation, it appears that not even the Prime Minister and his deputy could agree an appropriate way forward (see chapter 7, Race in Education). Consequently, it seems inevitable that colleges will continue to debate what to include in college policy, and what actions they should take regarding religion.

Chapter reflections

This chapter has considered what managing equality means for senior college managers; the significance of developing a contextually appropriate college equality policy; tutors' opportunities to engage with policy development; and tutors' personal responsibilities in policy implementation. The critical thinking tasks and case studies provided throughout the chapter should have enabled you to understand your role in these different situations.

Ofsted guidelines require colleges to actively engage with eliminating discrimination, promoting equal opportunities and to meet the diverse needs of all students (Ofsted, 2012, p 11) as a means of achieving social and educational inclusion (Ofsted, 2009, p 19). In addition colleges should tackle unlawful discrimination, inequality and unfairness and adopt practices that make best use of the differing skills and talents of individuals (ibid). LLUK state that college tutors should be actively committed to equality, diversity and inclusion in relation to learners, the workforce, and the community and should evaluate and develop [their] own practice in promoting equality ... and engaging with diversity' (2006, p 3). Further, the IfL encourages tutors to go beyond the legal requirements relating to equality (IfL, 2009, p 3). This is a significant challenge and requires the efforts, good will and creativity of students, staff and wider communities.

Equality can only be achieved when college managers have established a relevant policy framework and have created the conditions necessary for implementing their policies; when every college tutor has taken the time and personal responsibility to understand what equality policy means for them, their students and their college. Only when these conditions are achieved can equality become reality for all college users. Without everyone working together, it is unlikely that Ofsted's, LLUK's or IfL's grand ambitions will be realised. Promoting equality is, and must be, a whole college endeavour.

LEARNING REVIEW AUDIT

Topic	I feel confident in doing this	This is an area I will need to develop
I can state the responsibilities and roles of senior managers in developing effective equality and diversity practices		
I understand the process of policy implementation and my role within this		
I am aware of my individual organisational responsibilities as a tutor in FE		

Taking it further

Advisory, Conciliation and Arbitration Service (ACAS) (2011) *Delivering Equality and Diversity*. London: ACAS Publications.

Daniels, K and Macdonald, L (2005) *Equality, Diversity and Discrimination*. London: Chartered Institute of Personnel and Development.

Gravells, A and Simpson, S (2012) *Equality and Diversity in the Lifelong Learning Sector*. London: Sage/Learning Matters.

Kumra, S and Manfredi, S (2012) *Managing Equality and Diversity: Theory and Practice*. Oxford: Oxford University Press.

Thompson, N (2011) *Promoting Equality: Working with Diversity and Difference*. Basingstoke: Palgrave Macmillan.

www.csie.org.uk Centre for Studies on Inclusive Education

www.citizensadvice.org.uk Citizens Advice Bureau

www.ecu.ac.uk Equalities Challenge Unit

www.equalityhumanrights.com Equality and Human Rights Commission

References

Bush, T and Coleman M (2004) *Leadership and Strategic Management in Education*. London: Paul Chapman Publishing.

Dadzie, S (2004) *Toolkit for Tackling Racism in School*. Stoke: Trentham Books.

Department for Education and Skills (DfES) (2006) *Getting It, Getting It Right*. DfES.

Gillborn, D (1995) *Racism and Antiracism in Real Schools*. Buckingham: Open University Press.

IfL (2009) *Single Equality Strategy.* Available at www.ifl.ac.uk/media/53480/2014_01_01_IfL_single_equality_strategy.pdf Accessed 8 May 2014.

Kotter, J (2012) *Leading Change*. HBR Books: USA.

LLUK (2006) *New Overarching Professional Standards for Teachers, Tutors and Trainers in the Lifelong Learning Sector*. London: LLUK.

Ofsted (2005) *Race Equality in Further Education: A Report by HMI*. London: Ofsted.

Ofsted (2009) *Ofsted Inspects: A Framework for All Ofsted Inspection and Regulation*. London: Ofsted.

Ofsted (2012) *The Framework for School Inspection*. Manchester: Ofsted.

Ofsted (2014) *Handbook for the Inspection of Further Education and Skills*. Ofsted: Manchester.

Peart, S (2013) *Making Education Work: How Black Men and Boys Navigate the Further Education Sector*. London: Institute of Education Press.

Glossary of acronyms

A/AS level	Advanced/Advanced Subsidiary level
ACAS	Advisory, Conciliation and Arbitration Service
ASBO	Anti-Social Behaviour Order
ASE	Association for Science Education
ATL	Association of Teachers and Lecturers
ATLS	Associate Teacher Learning and Skills
BAME	Black, Asian and Minority Ethnic
BCS	British Computing Society
BHS	British Horse Society
BBC	British Broadcasting Company
BME	Black and Minority Ethnic
BTEC	Business and Technology Education Council
CAB	Citizens' Advice Bureau
CBI	Confederation for British Industry
CertEd	Certificate of Education
CRE	Commission for Racial Equality
DCSF	Department for Children, Schools and Families
DES	Department for Education and Science

DfE	Department for Education
DfEE	Department for Education and Employment
DfES	Department for Education and Skills
EEA	European Economic Area
EMDA	East Midlands Development Agency
ESA	Employment and Support Allowance
ESOL	English for Speakers of Other Languages
ESN	Educationally Sub Normal
EU	European Union
FdA	Foundation Degree
FE	Further Education
GCSE	General Certificate of Education
GTCE	General Teaching Council England
HBCUs	Historically Black Colleges and Universities
HNC	Higher National Certificate
HND	Higher National Diploma
HR	Human Resources
IfL	Institute for Learning
IFP	Increased Flexibility Programme
ILEA	Inner London Education Authority
INICO	Instituto Universitarios de Integracaion en la Comunidad
IVF	In Vitro Fertilisation
JSA	Jobseekers Allowance
LEA	Local Education Authority
LGBT	Lesbian, Gay, Bisexual and Transgender
LLUK	Lifelong Learning United Kingdom
LSIS	Learning and Skills Improvement Service
MMR	Measles, Mumps and Rubella

MOT	Motor Ordnance Test
NAACP	National Association for the Advancement of Colored People
NAO	National Audit Office
NEET	Not in Education Training or Employment
NHS	National Health Service
NIACE	National Institute for Adult and Continuing Education
NPS	National Probation Service
NQF	National Qualification Framework
NVQ	National Vocational Qualification
Ofsted	Office for Standards in Education
PGCE	Post Graduate Certificate of Education
ProfGCE	Professional Graduate Certificate of Education
QAA	Quality Assurance Agency
QCF	Qualification and Credit Framework
QTLS	Qualified Teacher Learning and Skills
RNPE	Revised National Policy on Education
SFA	Skills Funding Agency
UCAS	University Council Admissions Service
UCU	University and College Union
UKBA	United Kingdom Border Agency
UKCISA	United Kingdom Council for International Student Affairs
UN	United Nations
UNHCR	United Nations High Commissioner for Refugees
VQ	Vocational Qualification
WBL	Work Based Learning

Index

academic ability, 97
Adult Court, 100, 101
adult education, 38
    and external influences on tutors, 43–44
    Foster review, 39
    for individuals and employers, 38–39
    learning technologies, 45
    purpose of FE, 43
adult learners, 4
    characteristics of, 39–42
    decision making process, 40
    learning communities, 45
    learning technologies, use of, 45
    levels of understanding, 40
    needs of, 44–45
    purpose of teaching, 37–38
    with special educational needs, 30
    strategies to support, 44–45
adult teaching, assumptions for, 46
African Americans
    No Child Left Behind legislation, 19
    racial segregation in the US, 19
    right to integrated education, 17–19
African slaves, in England, 20
andragogy (theory of adult learning), 46, 51, 55
anti-Black riots (1958), London, 21, 87
anti-racism educational charity, 24
Anti-Social Behaviour Orders (ASBOs), 107
apprentices, 4, 77
    academic qualifications, 70
    career/employment decision, 71
    levels of study, 70
    National Vocational Qualifications (NVQs), 70
    in UK education system, 69
    vocational education, 69
    wages, 70
    working with, 69–70

assessment, 8, 28, 118, 119
Associate Teacher Learning and Skills (ATLS), 11
Association for Science Education (ASE), 11
asylum seekers, 4, 77. See also refugees
    bogus, 72
    global asylum applications, 72
    safe havens, 76
    working with, 71–73

behaviour
    student behaviour, 47
    tutor behaviour, 56–57
bilingual schools, 31
bind-overs, imposition of, 107
bi-sexuality, 122
Black people. See African Americans
Board of Education, 51
Boyle, Edmund, 21
Boyle's Law, 21
Boys into Books initiative (2007–08), 114
British Computing Society (BCS), 11
British Horse Society (BHS), 11
British Overseas Territories, 74
buddy system, 54

Cameron, David, 72, 88
career choices, 116–17
Caribbean Society, 75
Charter of Rights and Freedoms (1982), Canada, 31
Cheyney University, Pennsylvania, 19
Citizens' Advice Bureau, 91
citizenship rights, in Britain, 21
City and Guilds qualifications, 70
Civil Rights Act (1964), US, 19
classroom management, 8, 40
Coard, B., 22
code of conduct. See student code of conduct

Code of Professional Practice, 11
colonialism, impact of, 21
Commission for Racial Equality (CRE), UK, 22
communities of practice, 45
compensation, 107
Confederation for British Industry (CBI), 77
conflict of interests, 57
Constitution Act (1982), Canada, 31
corporal punishment
   abolition of, 52
   for enforcing discipline, 52
County Court, 100
court costs, 107
creative learning opportunities, 131
crime management, role of judicial agencies in, 98–101
criminal careers, risk factor in, 97
criminal lifestyle, 97
criminal responsibility in the UK, age of, 100
cross-cultural groups
   and college communities, 91–92
   cultural identity, 91
   cultural location, 87
   and equality legislation in the UK, 83–84
   meaning of, 81–82
   membership of, 87
   race in education, 88–89
Crown Court, 99–100, 101
culture, meaning of, 81–82
curfews, 106
curriculum, 37, 43, 51, 62, 76
cyber-bullying, 59

data management systems, 115
decision-making, 28, 40
Department for Children, Schools and Families (DCSF), 23, 114
Department for Communities and Local Government, 91
Department for Education and Employment (DfEE), 38
Disability Discrimination Act (1995), UK, 32, 84

East Midlands Development Agency (EMDA), 77
Education Act (1880), UK, 20
Education Act (1944), UK, 25, 27, 38, 52, 62
education and social networking sites, 57
education system, 18, 97
   apprenticeships, 69
   dependency model, 25
   discrimination against Black people, 17–19, 22
   elementary, 29
   equality and diversity policies, 6, 11
   progressive stages of, 25
   state education, 51
Eisenhower, President, 18
e-learning, 45
electronic monitoring. *See* tagging
elementary education, 29
Employment and Support Allowance (ESA), 73
End Racism This Generation' campaign, 24
English for Speakers of Other Languages (ESOL), 73

Equalities Act (2010), UK, 2, 3, 4, 28, 32, 83–84, 87, 119, 122, 123, 140
   characteristics protected by, 84
Equalities Challenge Unit, 115, 119
equality and diversity, in Further Education
   challenges associated with, 135–36
   college responses to, 129–31
   implementation of, 139
   minority perspectives, accommodation of, 140
   policy development and implementation, 132–33
equality of opportunity, 25
equality, concept of, 6, 24
European Economic Area (EEA), 74
European Union (EU). *See* European Economic Area (EEA)
extra-curricular activities, 19

Family Courts, 101
Faubus' school closure law, 18
FE colleges, 4, 11, 38, 103, 115, 125
   charter, 59
   curriculum, 37
   duty of care standards, 57–58
   equality and diversity in, 4
   equality policy, 130, 136, 140
   leadership and management, quality of, 131
   transition from school to, 52–54
FE tutors, 123
   adult education influence on, 43–44
   assessment of learner progress, 8
   behaviour, 56–57
   classroom management skills, 8
   Code of Professional Practice, 11
   equality and diversity, importance of, 6, 11
   legislative boundation, 3
   peer support, 13–14
   professional expectations, 8–9, 10
   residential trips, 7–8
   responsibilities, 4, 8–9, 10, 103, 137
   role conflict, 103–104
   subject knowledge of, 8
   teaching ability, 10
feedback, 45
femininity, normative models of, 118
fines, for offence in Further Education, 105
Finnish sign language, 31
Foundation Degrees (FdAs), 70

Gender Agenda initiative (2008–09), 114
gender and sexual orientation, issue of
   career choices, 116–17
   gender and achievement, 115
   gender and education debates, 113–14
   gender, expressions of, 123–25
      transgender students, 124–25
   ladette behaviour, 117–18
   male/female achievement and engagement, 113–14
   pregnancy and maternity, 119–21
   public reactions to pregnancy, 119
   sexuality, expressions of, 121–23

gender and sexual orientation, issue of (*cont.*)
    heterosexuality, 121–22
    homosexuality, 123–25
  teenage pregnancies, 19
gender dysphoria, 124
gender identity, 124
General Certificate of Education (GCSEs), 120
Gillborn, D., 129
government agencies, expectations of, 10–11

hepatitis, 75
heterosexuality, 121–22
High Court, 100
higher education, 29
Higher Education Act (1965), US, 19
Higher National Certificates (HNCs), 70
Higher National Diplomas (HNDs), 70
Historically Black Colleges and Universities (HBCUs), 19, 24
Home Office, 98, 99
homosexuality, 123–25
human rights, 30

Increased Flexibility Programme (IFP), 52, 53, 62
Inner London Education Authority (ILEA), 22
Institute for Learning (IfL), 3, 11
interactive human community, 82
international perspectives, on students with
    disabilities, 29–30

Jobseekers Allowance (JSA), 73
judicial agencies, role in crime management, 98–101
  Adult Court, 100
  County Court, 100
  Crown Court, 99–100
  Family Courts, 101
  High Court, 100
  Magistrates' Court, 100
  National Probation Service (NPS), 101
  police and security forces, 99
  Youth Court, 100–101
junior academies, 63

Kansas Board of Education, 18
Knowles, Malcolm, 46
Kotter, J., 132
  model of equality and diversity, 132–33

Lamb report, 28
laws and legislation
  Boyle's Law, 21
  Civil Rights Act (1964), US, 19
  Constitution Act (1982), Canada, 31
  Disability Discrimination Act (1995), UK, 32, 84
  Education Act (1880), UK, 20
  Education Act (1944), UK, 25, 27, 38, 52, 62
  Equalities Act (2010), UK, 2, 3, 4, 28–29, 32, 83–84,
    119, 122, 123, 140
  Higher Education Act (1965), US, 19
  No Child Left Behind legislation, 19

Race Relations Act (1965), UK, 32
Race Relations Act (1976), UK, 84
Sex Discrimination Act (1975), UK, 32, 84
Voting Rights Act (1965), US, 19
Learning and Skills Improvement Service (LSIS), 11
learning technologies, 45
LGBT (lesbian, gay, bi-sexual, transgender) groups, 123,
    134, 136, 137
Lifelong Learning UK (LLUK), 10
Little Rock Nine dispute, 3, 18–19
Local Education Authorities (LEAs), 52

Magistrates' Court, 100
Mechanics' Institutes, 38
  agendas of, 38
Merkel, Angela, 88
minority communities, 91
multicultural societies, 88–89
mumps and rubella (MMR), 75

National Association for the Advancement of Colored
    People (NAACP), 18
National Institute for Adult and Continuing Education
    (NIACE), 38
National Occupational Standards, 11
National Probation Service (NPS), 98, 101, 105, 106
National Vocational Qualifications (NVQs), 52, 62, 70
No Child Left Behind legislation, 19

offending, in Further Education
  background to, 96–98
  community sentences, 105–106
  custodial sentences, 105
    suspended, 105
  doing the right thing wrong, 104
  FE tutors, role conflict, 103–104
  fines, 105
  judicial agencies, roles of, 98–101
  offence, types of, 96
  other orders and requirements, 106–107
  personal responsibility factors, 97
  questionable offerings, 108–109
  reports of, 95
  second chance, 103
  sentencing options, 104–105
  societal factors, 97–98
  in the UK, 95–96
Ofsted, 6, 29, 115, 130, 131, 133, 139
overseas students, 4
  academic support, 75
  accommodation, 75
  banking services, 75
  educational goals and aspirations, 76
  escaping, 76–77
  friendship groups, 75
  health services, 75
  safe havens, 76
  vaccination, 75
  working with, 74–75

pedagogy (art and science of teaching children), 46
people with disabilities, 25
police and security forces, role in crime
        management, 99
policy, education, 11, 28, 140
    development of, 132–33
    on equality, 130
    implementation of, 91, 129, 132–33, 135
    on multiculturalism, 88
    'no phones in classroom policy', 47
    for primary education, 51
    significance of, 129
poverty, 98
Prison Reform Trust, 97
problem solving, 13, 135
professional responsibility, of FE staff, 4, 8–9, 10, 43, 65,
        76, 103, 119, 131, 137

Qualification and Credit Framework (QCF), 60
qualifications offered in schools, 60
Qualified Teacher Learning and Skills (QTLS), 3, 11
Quality Assurance Agency (QAA), 76

race and education, in the UK
    Black North Africans, 20
    Boyle's Law, 21
    British colonialism, impact of, 21
    colonial migrants, 21
    education at British universities, 21
    equality, promotion of, 24
    and global perspectives on racism, 24
    history of, 20–26
    progressive stages of education, 25
    racial segregation, 21
    racial tension, in the UK, 21–22
    responses to disability in education
        dependency model, 25
        Equality Act (2010), 28–29
        Lamb report, 28
        Tomlinson report, 27–28
        towards entitlement, 26
        Warnock report, 27
    schooling of Black children, 22
    segregation, stereotyping and schooling, 22–23
    slavery, abolition of, 20
race and education, in the US
    African Americans. See African Americans
    discrimination against Black people, 17
    equality, principle of, 17
    history of, 17–19
    Little Rock Nine dispute, 18–19
    No Child Left Behind legislation, 19
    racial segregation in schools, 18
    slave trade, 17
Race Relations Act (1965), UK, 32
Race Relations Act (1976), UK, 84
racial discrimination
    in education, 17–19, 21
    in employment, 19, 21

    in schools, 18
racial tension, in the UK, 21–22
racism, global perspectives on, 24
Raising Boys' Achievements project, 114
Rampton, Anthony, 22
Refugee Council, 76
refugees, 4
    country of origin, 72
    definition of, 71
    working with, 71–73
residential trips, 7–8
Revised National Policy on Education (RNPE),
        Botswana, 30
right to education, 29
Runneymede Trust, 24

Salamanca conference (1994), 3, 30, 32
School Library Association (SLA), 114
school–college transition, 52–54
segregated schooling, idea of, 18, 22, 24
self control, lack of, 97
self-concept, 63
self-esteem, 63
self-supporting learners, 48
Severus, Septimius, 20
Sex Discrimination Act (1975), UK, 32, 84
sex education, 114
sexual attraction, 122
sexual difference, social and cultural aspects of, 123
Show Racism the Red Card' organisation, 24
Skills Funding Agency (SFA), 72
slave trade, 17
slavery, abolition of, 20
social exclusion, 24
special educational needs, 30
staff–student relationships, 7
starting teaching, 10
state multiculturalism, doctrine of, 88
student behaviour, 47
student charters, 59, 64
student code of conduct, 59, 64, 65
student integration, academic and social, 64–65
students with disabilities, 6, 27
    decision making processes, 28
    education for, 32
    international perspectives on, 29–30
    responses to
        Equality Act (2010), UK, 28–29
        Lamb report, 28
        Tomlinson report, 27–28
        Warnock report, 27
    rights of, 29
students' union, 115
subject knowledge, 8
Swann Report, 3, 22
Swann, Michael, 22

tagging, 106
teacher training course, 40

teaching
methods of, 41
starting, 10
teaching abilities, 10
teaching organisations, expectations of, 10–11
teaching unions, 3, 11, 13
Think Global, Act Local, concept of, 24
Tomlinson report, 27–28
Tomlinson, John, 27
transgender students, 124–25
transient populations
career choices, 71
financial gain, 71
vocational education, 69
working with
apprentices, 69–70
overseas students, 74–75
refugees and asylum seekers, 71–73

UK Civil Rights movement, 19
UN Universal Declaration of Human Rights, 29
United Kingdom Border Agency (UKBA), 74
United Kingdom Council for International Student Affairs
(UKCISA), 75, 76
United Nations High Commissioner for Refugees (UNHCR), 71
University and College Union (UCU), 11, 12
US Civil Rights movement, 3, 18, 19

vaccination, of overseas students, 75
values and teaching in FE, 55
vocational learning, 52

Vocational Qualifications (VQ), 60, 62
vocational training, 38, 69
Voting Rights Act (1965), US, 19

wages, 70
Warnock Report, 3, 27
Warnock, Mary, 27
recommendations for FE, 27
work based learning (WBL), 60

young and younger learners in colleges
academic and social integration of, 64–65
background of, 51–52
buddy system, 54
building relationships and maintaining professional
boundaries, 54–55
code of conduct, 59, 64, 65
duty of care, 57–58
entitlements and responsibilities, 59
impact on learning, 63
induction programme, 54
modes of study available to, 62–63
personal tutors, 54
qualifications available to, 60–62
safety issues, 58–59
school–college transition, managing, 52–54
signpost students and information points, 54
tutor behaviour, 56–57
Youth Court, 100–101
youth unemployment, 117
YouTube, 58